Hands-on Go Programming

*Learn Google's Golang Programming,
Data Structures, Error Handling and
Concurrency*

Sachchidanand Singh
Prithvipal Singh

www.bpbonline.com

FIRST EDITION 2021

Copyright © BPB Publications, India

ISBN: 978-93-89898-19-4

Distributors:

BPB PUBLICATIONS
20, Ansari Road, Darya Ganj
New Delhi-110002
Ph: 23254990/23254991

DECCAN AGENCIES
4-3-329, Bank Street,
Hyderabad-500195
Ph: 24756967/24756400

MICRO MEDIA
Shop No. 5, Mahendra Chambers,
150 DN Rd. Next to Capital Cinema,
V.T. (C.S.T.) Station, MUMBAI-400 001
Ph: 22078296/22078297

BPB BOOK CENTRE
376 Old Lajpat Rai Market,
Delhi-110006
Ph: 23861747

To View Complete
BPB Publications Catalogue
Scan the QR Code:

Published by Manish Jain for BPB Publications, 20 Ansari Road, Darya Ganj, New Delhi-110002 and Printed by him at Repro India Ltd, Mumbai

www.bpbonline.com

Dedicated to

My Parents, Wife Nirmala
&
Loving Daughter Anvi and Son Vansh
— Sachchidanand Singh

My Parents, Wife Rajani
&
Loving son Parthiv
— Prithvipal Singh

About the Authors

Mr. Sachchidanand Singh is working as Advanced Analytics, BI and Data Science SME at IBM India Software Labs (ISL), Pune. He is M.Tech from the Birla Institute of Technology and Science (BITS), Pilani. He has authored more than a dozen technical research papers in IEEE, international computer journals, and national/international conferences.

He holds several patents in Artificial Intelligence, Machine Learning, Cloud and Cognitive domain. He has rich experience in architecture design and solution implementation with technologies like Advanced Analytics and Business Intelligence (BI). He is an IEEE reviewer, Technical Program Committee (TPC) member of various national/international conferences, and a review board member of the American Journal of Computer Science and Information Engineering, USA.

Mr. Prithvipal Singh has been working in the IT industry for nearly a decade. He has vast experience working in Java, Golang, Spring, Node.js, and Python. He has expertise in microservice architecture and the cloud domain. He has an MCA from Savitribai Phule Pune University.

About the Reviewer

Dolly Talreja is currently working as the technical lead and core member of a team developing 5G Core network (Golang Linux) and is an integral part of Altran Technologies. In her capacity, she is the owner of the nodes UDM and AUSF and is involved in completing SDLC. She is also an expert in analyzing network traces. She is part of a team that is at the forefront of innovation to address the entire breadth of the clients' opportunities in the evolving world of cloud and digital platforms. She is the alumni of NIT Warangal, with more than 6 years of experience in the industry, was the Lead Engineer at HP and played a key role in the development of LEDM. She is the owner of the Scan to Feature of HP. She was also part of the Samsung R&D Institute of India as the Senior Software Engineer and was part of a team developing SMB 3.0 protocol for Samsung's MPF. She also has to her credit a published paper in IEEE on decentralized peer-to-peer networks.

Acknowledgments

At this movement of my substantial enhancement, before we get into the thick of the things, we would like to add a few heartfelt words for the people who gave their unending support with their unfair humor and warm wishes. First and foremost, praises and thanks to the God, the Almighty, for his showers of blessings throughout in completing this book successfully.

We want to acknowledge our colleagues who provided us with the impetus to write a more suitable text. We are thankful to the management, seniors and colleagues for constantly keeping on pushing us to move higher and higher. Besides them, we thank all our friends, well-wishers, respondents, and academicians who helped us throughout our journey from the inception to the completion.

Preface

Golang is regarded as a swift and flawless programming language having loads of useful features like efficient built-in concurrency, garbage collector with automatic garbage detection and cleaning, dynamic growable call stack of goroutines, extremely fast compiler and cross platform versatility, etc. A lot of cloud, networking, and DevOps softwares are written in Golang like Docker, Kubernetes, Terraform, etcd, and ist.io. The Go developers community is one of the most active open source communities on GitHub.

This book focuses on learning Golang, starting from the basic concepts to interfaces, pointers, concurrency, etc. We have explained each concept in detail using programming examples. We start with the basics and get into more complex stuff with each chapter. Each chapter has exercises which will help you in understanding the concepts clearly.

Over the 12 chapters in this book, you will learn the following:

Chapter 1: [Introduction]

This chapter covers the basic concepts of data types, constants, variables, operators, reassignment, and redeclaration. You will learn how to use them in the Go programming language.

Chapter 2: [Functions]

This chapter will cover the function declaration, parameters, multiple returns, variadic function, and defer statement. It will also cover the concept of call by value and how to pass the address of the variable as a value.

Chapter 3: [Control flows]

The objective of this chapter is to introduce the concepts of control flows and loops to the readers and show how to use them.

Chapter 4: [Arrays]

The objective of this chapter is to introduce the concept of arrays to the readers. It will also show how to declare and initialize arrays, and pass arrays to function.

Chapter 5: [Slices]

The objective of this chapter is to introduce the concept of slices to the readers and tell them how to declare slices, the various ways of creating slices, modifying and comparing slices, about multi-dimensional slices, sorting slices, and iterate over slices.

Chapter 6: [Maps]

This chapter explains the basic concept of map and how to use it in the Go programming language. It covers how to declare and initialize a map, iterate over a map, how to perform retrieve, update, and delete over the map, and how to check if a key exists in a map, etc.

Chapter 7: [Structs]

This chapter explains the basic concept of struct and how to use it in the Go programming language. It covers how to declare and initialize structs type, access fields of structs, pointer to structs, exported and unexported structs, and structs fields.

Chapter 8: [Methods]

This chapter covers the concept of methods in the Go programming language. You will learn how to declare a method, how to call a method, the syntax of different types of methods, and the method resolution process.

Chapter 9: [Interfaces]

This chapter will cover the concept of interface in Golang. You will learn what the interface in Golang is, how Golang interfaces are different from other languages, how to declare an interface, and how implicit implementation happens in Golang and what are its benefits. We will create the interface without methods and see its benefits with built-in functions. We will see the impact of value receiver and pointer receiver while implementing the interface and creating polymorphic objects.

Chapter 10: [Pointers]

In this chapter, you will learn what pointers in Golang are. This chapter will explain to you the use of pointers, how to declare a pointer variable, and you will understand the pointer types. You will also learn why arithmetic operations are not allowed on pointer variables in Golang.

Chapter 11: [Concurrency]

This chapter will cover goroutines and channels. You will learn how to define a goroutine, what WaitGroup is, and how to use the WaitGroup to wait for other goroutines to finish. You will understand the concept of channel. We will use the channel for communication between the goroutines. We will create two types of goroutines: buffered and unbuffered.

Chapter 12: [Error handling]

This chapter will cover error handling. At the end of this chapter, you will learn what an error in Golang is, how to return an error from a function or method, and how to handle these errors in the caller function. We will also see a built-in error interface, the error packages and the method, function, and struct in the errors package. You will learn how to define a new error, create a customized error type, what panic is, how to handle panic using recover, what defer is, and the importance of the defer function while handling panic, etc.

Downloading the coloured images:

Please follow the link to download the
Coloured Images of the book:

https://rebrand.ly/xqrsibm

Errata

We take immense pride in our work at BPB Publications and follow best practices to ensure the accuracy of our content to provide with an indulging reading experience to our subscribers. Our readers are our mirrors, and we use their inputs to reflect and improve upon human errors if any, occurred during the publishing processes involved. To let us maintain the quality and help us reach out to any readers who might be having difficulties due to any unforeseen errors, please write to us at:

errata@bpbonline.com

Your support, suggestions and feedbacks are highly appreciated by the BPB Publications' Family.

BPB is searching for authors like you

If you're interested in becoming an author for BPB, please visit **www.bpbonline.com** and apply today. We have worked with thousands of developers and tech professionals, just like you, to help them share their insight with the global tech community. You can make a general application, apply for a specific hot topic that we are recruiting an author for, or submit your own idea.

The code bundle for the book is also hosted on GitHub at **https://github.com/bpbpublications/Hands-on-Go-programming**. In case there's an update to the code, it will be updated on the existing GitHub repository.

We also have other code bundles from our rich catalog of books and videos available at **https://github.com/bpbpublications**. Check them out!

PIRACY

If you come across any illegal copies of our works in any form on the internet, we would be grateful if you would provide us with the location address or website name. Please contact us at **business@bpbonline.com** with a link to the material.

If you are interested in becoming an author

If there is a topic that you have expertise in, and you are interested in either writing or contributing to a book, please visit **www.bpbonline.com**.

REVIEWS

Please leave a review. Once you have read and used this book, why not leave a review on the site that you purchased it from? Potential readers can then see and use your unbiased opinion to make purchase decisions, we at BPB can understand what you think about our products, and our authors can see your feedback on their book. Thank you!

For more information about BPB, please visit **www.bpbonline.com**.

Table of Contents

CHAPTER 1
Introduction

The Go programming language was conceived by Robert Griesemer, Rob Pike, and Ken Thompson in 2007 at Google. It's an open-source, general-purpose programming language that supports high-performance networking and multiprocessing. The Go compiler was initially written in C but it is now written in Go itself.

Structure

- Data types
- Constants, variables, and operators
- Typed constants and untyped constants
- Multiple constant declarations
- Redeclaration concept
- Reassignment concept
- Code structure

Objective

This chapter covers the basic concepts of data types, constants, variables, operators, reassignment, and redeclaration. You will learn how to use them in the Go programming language.

Introduction

Go is a systems-level programming language for large distributed systems and highly scalable network servers. It's well-suited for building infrastructures like networked servers and tools and is suitable for cloud, mobile applications, machine learning, etc. Go provides efficient concurrency, flexible approach to data abstraction, and supports automatic memory management, i.e., garbage collection.

Why Go programming?

Multithreading is supported by most of the programming languages, but race conditions and deadlocks create difficulties in creating the multithreaded application. For example, creating a new thread in Java consumes approximately 1 MB of the memory heap size. Now, consider a case wherein you need to spin thousands of such threads. Then, it will create out of memory.

Moreover, there is a limit to the number of cores you can add to the processors like quad-core and octa-core to increase processing power. You cannot keep on adding more cache to the processor in order to boost performance since there is a cost involved. Therefore, we are left with only one option to build a more efficient software having high performance.

Go provides a solution to the problem with goroutines. You can spin millions of them at a time since they consume ~2KB heap memory. Goroutines have faster startup time and they use more memory on a need basis only. Also, a single goroutine can run on multiple threads since goroutines and OS threads don't have 1:1 mapping.

1.1 Data types

Data types categorize a set of related values and describe the operations that can be performed.

1.1.1 Numeric types

They are arithmetic types and represent either integer types or floating-point values.

Integer types:

`uint8`	Unsigned 8-bit integers (0 to 255)
`uint16`	Unsigned 16-bit integers (0 to 65535)
`uint32`	Unsigned 32-bit integers (0 to 4294967295)
`uint64`	Unsigned 64-bit integers (0 to 18446744073709551615)
`int8`	Signed 8-bit integers (-128 to 127)
`int16`	Signed 16-bit integers (-32768 to 32767)
`int32`	Signed 32-bit integers (-2147483648 to 2147483647)
`int64`	Signed 64-bit integers (-9223372036854775808 to 9223372036854775807)

Table 1.1

Float types:

`float32`	IEEE-754 32-bit floating-point numbers
`float64`	IEEE-754 64-bit floating-point numbers
`complex64`	Complex numbers with float32 real and imaginary parts
`complex128`	Complex numbers with float64 real and imaginary parts

Table 1.2

1.1.2 String types

Strings are immutable types. This means that once created, you can't change the contents of a string. Go supports two styles of string literals: the double-quote style and the back-quote style.

String literals can be created using double quotes, `"Go Programming"` or backticks, `'Go Programming'`. With regular double-quoted strings, the special sequences like newlines are interpreted as actual newlines while escape sequences are ignored in the backtick character and treated as normal values. For example, \n gets replaced with a newline in double-quoted strings as shown below:

```
Program 1.1

//Go program showing newline sequence


package main


import "fmt"
```

```go
func main() {
    // newline sequence is treated as a special value
    x := "apple\norange"
    fmt.Println(x)

    // newline sequence is treated as two raw characters
    y := `apple\norange`
    fmt.Println(y)
}
```

The following will be the output for the above program:

apple

orange

apple\norange

1.1.3 Boolean types

Program 1.2

```go
//Go program to explain boolen types

package main

import "fmt"

func main() {
    var b bool
    fmt.Println(b)
    b = true
    fmt.Println(b)
}
```

The following will be the output for the above program:

false

true

1.1.4 Derived types

The derived type may include structure types, function types, slice types, interface types, map types, and channel types.

1.2 Constants

In Go, const is a keyword that introduces a name for a scalar value like 3.14159. Such values are called constants.

Type inference: When a variable is declared without specifying an explicit type (either by using the := syntax or the var = expression syntax), the variable's type is inferred from the value on the right-hand side.

Constants:

- Constants are declared with the const keyword and can be a numeric, string, Boolean, or character values.

- Constants cannot be declared using the := syntax

E.g.: const Pi = 3.14

1.2.1 Variable declaration

Variables declared without an explicit initial value are assigned the default zero value for numeric types, false for boolean types, and "" (the empty string) for string types. Let's look at the following program:

Program 1.3

```
//Go program showing variables declared
//without an explicit initial value

package main

import "fmt"

func main() {

    var f float64
    var i int
```

```
    var b bool
    var s string
    fmt.Printf("%v %v %v %q\n", f, i, b, s)
}
```

The following will be the output for the above program:

0 0 false ""

- In Go, the type of a variable is specified after the variable name.
- If you want to put two (or more) statements on one line, they must be separated with a semicolon (;).
- When declaring a variable, it is assigned the *natural* null value for the type.
- This means that here, after var i int, i has a value of 0.
- With var s string, s is assigned the zero string which is "".

Compare the following pieces of code which have the same effect:

Declaration with =

```
var a int = 20
var b bool = true
```

The var keyword is used to declare a variable and then assign a value to it.

Declaration with :=

You can drop var and data-type in this syntax.

```
a := 20
b := true
```

When Go finds the := assignment syntax, it understands that a new variable needs to be declared with an initial value. But you cannot use this syntax to assign a value to a pre-defined variable. The variable type is deduced from the value. For example, a value of 20 indicates an int and a value of true tells Go that the type should be Boolean.

1.2.2 Short variable declaration

In Go, you can declare variables in the following two ways:

- Using var keyword
- Using a short declaration operator (:=)

The short variable declaration operator (:=) is used to declare and initialize the local variables inside a function. It narrows the scope of the variable.

Using a short declaration operator, variables are declared without specifying the type. The type of variable is determined by the type of expression on the right-hand side of the := operator.

Syntax of short variable declaration operator:

```
variable_name := expression or value
```

Examples:

```
a := 10
x, y := 100, 200
p, q, r := 150, 250, 300
```

Short variable declaration:

- It is used to declare and initialize variables inside a function only.
- The variable declaration and initialization are made at the same time.
- Variables are declared inside the function, hence they have local scope.
- It is not required to mention the type of the variable in the short variable declaration.

1.3 Operator

Operators are used to performing the given mathematical or logical calculations. The following built-in operators are supported by Golang:

- Arithmetic operators
- Relational operators
- Logical operators
- Bitwise operators
- Assignment operators
- Miscellaneous operators

1.3.1 Arithmetic operators

Refer to the following table:

+	Adds two operands
-	Subtracts the second operand from the first operand
*	Multiplies both operands
/	Divides numerator by denominator
%	Modulus operator. It gives the remainder after an integer division
++	Increment operator. It increases the integer value by one
- -	Decrement operator. It decreases the integer value by one

Table 1.3

1.3.2 Relational operators

Refer to the following table:

==	It checks if the values of two operands are equal or not. If yes, then the condition becomes true
!=	It checks if the values of two operands are equal or not. If the values are not equal, then the condition becomes true
>	It checks if the value of the left operand is greater than the value of the right operand. If yes, then the condition becomes true
<	It checks if the value of the left operand is less than the value of the right operand or not. If yes, then the condition becomes true
>=	It checks if the value of the left operand is greater than or equal to the value of the right operand. If yes, then the condition becomes true
<=	It checks if the value of the left operand is less than or equal to the value of the right operand. If yes, then the condition becomes true

Table 1.4

1.3.2.1 Logical operators

Refer to the following table:

&&	Logical AND operator
||	Logical OR operator
!	It is called logical NOT operator and is used to reverse the logical state of its operand. If a condition is true, then the Logical NOT operator will make it false

Table 1.5

Program 1.4

```go
// Go program to explain logical operators
package main

import "fmt"

func main() {
    var a int = 10
    var b int = 20

    // logical AND operators
    if a != b && a <= b {
    fmt.Println("True")
    }

    // logical OR operators
    if a != b || a <= b {
    fmt.Println("True")
    }

    // logical NOT operators
    if !(a == b) {
    fmt.Println("True")
```

```
    }

}
```

We will get the following output:

True

True

True

1.3.2.2 Bitwise operators

Bitwise operators work on bits and perform a bit-by-bit operation. Refer to the following table:

&	Binary AND Operator copies a bit to the result if it exists in both operands
|	Binary OR Operator copies a bit if it exists in either operand
^	Binary XOR Operator copies the bit if it is set in one operand, but not both

Table 1.6

Truth tables for &, |, and ^ are given below:

x	Y	x & y	p | q	P ^ q
0	0	0	0	0
0	1	0	1	1
1	1	1	1	0
1	0	0	1	1

Table 1.7

1.3.2.3 Assignment operators

Refer to the following table:

=	A simple assignment operator assigns values from the right side operands to the left side operand
+=	Add AND assignment operator: It adds the right operand to the left operand and assigns the result to the left operand
-=	Subtract AND assignment operator: It subtracts the right operand from the left operand and assigns the result to the left operand

*=	Multiply AND assignment operator: It multiplies the right operand with the left operand and assigns the result to the left operand
/=	Divide AND assignment operator: It divides the left operand with the right operand and assigns the result to the left operand
%=	Modulus AND assignment operator: It takes the modulus using two operands and assigns the result to the left operand
<<=	Left shift AND assignment operator
>>=	Right shift AND assignment operator
&=	Bitwise AND assignment operator
^=	Bitwise exclusive OR and assignment operator
|=	Bitwise inclusive OR and assignment operator

Table 1.8

Program 1.5

```
// Go program to explain Left shift AND assignment operator
package main

import (
    "fmt"
)

func main() {
    var a, b uint
    a, b = 1, 1

    for b = 1; b < 5; b++ {
        fmt.Printf("%d << %d = %d \n", a, b, a<<b)
    }
}
```

We will get the following output:

```
1 << 1 = 2
1 << 2 = 4
1 << 3 = 8
```

```
1 << 4 = 16
```

Program 1.6
```
// Go program to explain Right shift AND assignment operator
package main

import (
    "fmt"
)

func main() {
    var a, b uint
    a, b = 512, 1

    for b = 1; b < 5; b++ {
    fmt.Printf("%d >> %d = %d \n", a, b, a>>b)
    }
}
```

We will get the following output:
```
512 >> 1 = 256
512 >> 2 = 128
512 >> 3 = 64
512 >> 4 = 32
```

Program 1.7
```
/* Go program to explain bitwise AND assignment operator,
   bitwise exclusive OR and assignment operator and
   bitwise inclusive OR and assignment operator */
package main

import "fmt"
```

```
func main() {
    var a, b, c int //default value of a, b, c is 0


    a &= 2 //Its same as a = a & 2, here & is Binary AND Operator
    fmt.Printf("Example of &= Operator: value of a = %d\n", a)


    b ^= 2 //Its same as b = b ^ 2, here ^ is Binary XOR Operator
    fmt.Printf("Example of ^= Operator: value of b = %d\n", b)


    c |= 2 //Its same as c = c | 2, here | is Binary OR Operator
    fmt.Printf("Example of |= Operator: value of c = %d\n", c)
}
```

We will get the following output:

Example of &= Operator: value of a = 0

Example of ^= Operator: value of b = 2

Example of |= Operator: value of c = 2

1.4 Typed constants and untyped constants

The type of each variable in Go is inferred by the compiler at the compile time. Therefore, Go is called a statically typed programming language. Go doesn't allow performing operations that mix numeric types. For example, you cannot add an int variable to int64 variable as shown below:

```
var x int = 100
var y int64 = 200


var sum = x + y // It will give compiler error
```

The above operation will give compiler error as you are trying to add int variable with the int64 variable. You need to explicitly cast variables so that they are of the same type to perform an operation like addition, subtraction, etc. as shown below:

```
var a int = 10
var b int64 = 20


var sum = a + int(b)    // It's allowed and works
```

1.4.1 Typed constants

In Go, any constant is typed if its type is explicitly mentioned. For example:

```
const x float64 = 9.75  //It's types constant
const x int = 10        //It's types constant
```

1.4.2 Untyped constants

In Go, any constant (named or unnamed) is untyped if its type is explicitly not mentioned. For example:

```
20        // untyped integer constant
"Golang"  // untyped string constant
false     // untyped boolean constant
```

1.5 Multiple constant declarations

We can declare multiple constants in one statement and multiple variables of a single type in a single statement. For example:

```
const x, y, z int = 10, 20, 30
```

1.6 Redeclaration concept

If a variable is already declared, you cannot redeclare that variable in the same block. The redeclaration just assigns a new value to the original value as shown below:

```
Program 1.8

//Go redeclaration concept


package main


import "fmt"


func main() {
    a := 10
    a := 20
    fmt.Println(a)
}
```

We will get the following output:

no new variables on left side of :=

You can redeclare variables using short multi-variable declarations where at least one new variable is introduced as shown below:

Program 1.9

```
//Go program for short multi-variable declarations


package main


import "fmt"


func main() {
    a := 10
    a, b := 20, 30
    fmt.Println("value of a:", a)
    fmt.Println("value of b:", b)
}
```

We will get the following output:

value of a: 20

value of b: 30

1.7 Reassignment concept

You can perform reassignment of variables in Golang. The set of values allowed to store in a variable are determined by the variable's type. The rule which is used to govern the permitted values is called assignability. Let's look at the following example:

Program 1.10

```
//Go reassignment concept


package main


import "fmt"
```

```go
func main() {
    x := 10
    {
        fmt.Println("value of x:", x)
        //new local variable x
        x, y := 20, 30
        fmt.Println("value of x:", x)
        fmt.Println("value of y:", y)
    }
    fmt.Println("value of x:", x)
}
```

We will get the following output:

value of x: 10

value of x: 20

value of y: 30

value of x: 10

In Program 1.5, variable x has been shadowed due to x, y := 20, 30. The value of x, outside the inner scope, remained the same, i.e., 10 and inside the scope, it was 20 after it was shadowed.

1.8 Code structure

Go programs are constructed using several packages for efficient management of the dependencies. The following is a sample Go program with the print statement:

Program 1.11

```go
//Sample Go program


package main


import "fmt"


func main() {
```

```
    fmt.Println("Let us GO")
}
```

To run the program, put the code in a file having the name suffix with `.go`, something like `first-program.go`, and then hit the following command.

```
$ go run first-program.go
```

Output 1.6

Let us GO

Conclusion

- Golang is an open-source, general-purpose programming language that supports high-performance networking and multiprocessing, etc.

- Go is well-suited for building infrastructures like networked servers and tools, and is also suitable for cloud, mobile applications, and machine learning.

- Goroutines have faster startup time and they use extra memory on a need basis only. Also, a single goroutine can run on multiple threads since goroutines and OS threads don't have 1:1 mapping.

- Go supports data types like numeric types, string types, boolean types, derived types, etc.

- Golang provides built-in relational operators, arithmetic operators, logical operators, bitwise operators, assignment operators, etc.

- The type of every variable in Go is inferred by the compiler at compile time. Hence, Go is called a statically typed programming language.

- You can redeclare variables using short multi-variable declarations where at least one new variable is introduced.

- Go programs are constructed using several packages for efficient management of dependencies.

Questions

1. What is Golang and what are its benefits?
2. How can we print the type of a variable in Golang?
3. What are Goroutines? Explain the benefits of using them.
4. What is the static type declaration of a variable in Golang?
5. What are typed constants and untyped constants?

6. What is the difference between = and := operator?

7. What is a string literal in Golang?

8. What are packages in Golang?

9. What is the default value of a local variable in Golang?

10. What is the static type variable declaration in Golang?

11. How do we find the length of a string in Golang?

12. What is the string data type in Golang? Can you change a specific character in a string?

CHAPTER 2
Functions

Functions in Go are a set of statements which perform a task together. Every Go program will have one main(). Functions help you to divide big tasks into smaller pieces of code and improve readability and maintainability of the program.

Structure

- Function declaration
- Parameters and returns
- Multiple returns and named return
- Call by value
- Variadic functions
- Defer
- Programming examples

Objective

This chapter will cover function declaration, parameters, multiple returns, the variadic function, and defer statement. It will also cover the concept of call by value and how to pass address of the variable as a value. You will learn how to use them in the Go programming language.

2.1 Function

A function is an independent section of code that maps input parameters to output parameters. It is a collection of statements that are used to perform a specific task and return the result to the caller.

Functions are the building blocks of a Go program. They have inputs, outputs, and a series of steps called statements that are executed in order.

2.1.1 Function declarations

A function declaration consists of the keyword func, the name of the function, a parameter list (empty for main), a result list (also empty here), and the body of the function—the statements that define what it does—enclosed in braces.

Function declaration has a name, a list of parameters, an optional list of results, and a body as shown below:

```
func name ( parameter-list )( result-list ){
    //body of the function
}
```

2.2 Parameters and returns

The function definition in Go programming language is as follows:

```
func function_name( [parameter_list] ) [return_types] {
    //Body of function
}
```

2.2.1 Parameters

When a function is invoked, you pass a value to the parameter. A parameter is like a placeholder. This value is referred to as an actual parameter or argument. The parameter list refers to the type, order, and the number of the parameters of a function. Parameters are optional in functions. Hence, a function may contain no parameters.

2.2.2 Returns

A function may return a list of values. The return_types is the list of data types of the values that the function returns. Some functions perform the desired operations without returning a value. In this case, the return_type is not required.

Here is a sample Go program to explain parameters and returns:

Program 2.1

```go
// Go program to explain parameters and returns


package main


import "fmt"


func main() {
    /* declare local variables*/
    var x int = 50
    var y int = 40
    var sum_value int

    /* calling a function to get sum of values */
    sum_value = sum(x, y)

    fmt.Printf("Sum value is: %d\n", sum_value)
}


/* function returns the sum of two numbers */
func sum(num1, num2 int) int {
    /* declare local variables */
    var result int
    result = num1 + num2
    return result
}
```

The following will be the output for the above program:

```
Sum value is: 90
```

While creating a Go function, you define the task that the function will perform. To use a function, you will have to call that function to perform the predefined task.

When a program calls a function, the program control is transferred to the called function. A called function performs a defined task, and when its return statement is executed or when its function-ending closing brace is reached, it returns the program control to the main program.

To call a function, you simply need to pass the required parameters along with its function name. If the function returns a value, then you can store the returned value.

2.3 Multiple returns and named return

Golang allows giving names to the return or result parameters of the functions in the function definition. Also, Go has built-in support for multiple return values. This feature is used to return both result and error values from a function.

2.3.1 Multiple returns

In Go, a function can return multiple values using the `return` statement. The type of return values depends on the type of the parameters defined in the parameter list as shown below:

```
Program 2.2
// Go program to explain multiple returns
package main


import "fmt"


// testfunc return 2 values of int type
func testfunc(x, y int) (int, int) {
    return x + y, x - y
}


func main() {
```

```
    // Return values are assigned into different variables
    var testvar1, testvar2 = testfunc(10, 20)


    fmt.Printf("addition result: %d", testvar1)
    fmt.Printf("\nsubtraction result: %d", testvar2)
}
```

The following will be the output for the above program:

addition result: 30

subtraction result: -10

2.3.2 Named returns

Golang allows giving names to the return parameters of the functions in the function definition, i.e., explicit naming of return variables in the function definition. It eliminates the need to mention the variable's name with the `return` statement.

This concept is generally used when a function needs to return multiple values. Golang provides this facility for the user's comfort and to enhance the code readability.

Syntax for named returns:

```
func func_name(Par-list)(result_par1 data_type, result_par2 data_type,
....){
    // function body


    return
}
```

Let's see an example:

Program 2.3

```
// Golang program to show the use of named return arguments


package main


import "fmt"
```

```go
// Main Method
func main() {

    // calling the function which returns one values
    x := sum(10, 20)

    fmt.Println("10 + 20 =", x)
}


// function with named arguments
func sum(a, b int) (add int) {
    add = a + b

    // return keyword without any resultant parameters
    return
}
```

The following will be the output for the above program:

```
10 + 20 = 30
```

2.4 Call by value

Golang supports call by value to pass arguments to the function. Go does not have a call by reference since it doesn't have reference variables. However, we can pass the address of the variable as a value. Golang uses, by default, the call by value way to pass the arguments to the function.

2.4.1 Call by value

The call by value method of passing arguments to a function copies the actual value of an argument into the formal parameter of the function. The values of the actual parameters are copied to the function's formal parameters, and the two types of parameters are stored in different memory locations. The changes made to the parameter inside the function do not affect the argument, i.e., the changes made inside the functions are not reflected in the actual parameters of the caller:

```
Program 2.4
```

```go
// Go program to explain call by value
package main

import "fmt"

// function to change the value of given variable
func replace(x int) {
    x = 20
}

// main function
func main() {

    var x int = 10
    fmt.Printf("value of x before function call = %d", x)

    // call by value
    replace(x)
    fmt.Printf("\nvalue of x after function call = %d", x)
}
```

The following will be the output for the above program:

value of x before function call = 10

value of x after function call = 10

As discussed earlier, Go does not have a call by reference since it doesn't have reference variables. However, we can pass the address of the variable as a value. Here, we will use the concept of pointers and dereference operators. The address operator, & is used to get the address of a variable of any data type and the dereference operator, * is used to access the value at an address.

Since the actual and formal parameters refer to the same locations, any changes made inside the function are reflected in the actual parameters of the caller. This is shown below:

Program 2.5

```go
// Go program to explain call by passing the address of the variable
```

```
package main

import "fmt"

// function to change the value of given variable
func replace(x *int) {
    *x = 20
}


// main function
func main() {

    var x int = 10
    fmt.Printf("value of x before function call = %d", x)

    // call by reference
    replace(&x)
    fmt.Printf("\nvalue of x after function call = %d", x)
}
```

The following will be the output for the above program:

```
value of x before function call = 10
value of x after function call = 20
```

2.5 Variadic functions

Functions, in general, accept only a fixed number of arguments but the variadic function can accept a variable number of arguments.

Only the last parameter of a function can be variadic. If the last parameter of a function definition is prefixed by an ellipsis (. . .), then the function can accept any number of arguments for that parameter. This is shown as follows:

```
func variadic_function(a int, b ...int) {
    // Body of variadic function
}
```

In the above function, the parameter b is variadic since it's prefixed by an ellipsis, and it can accept any number of arguments.

Let's make the first parameter of the `variadic_function` variadic. The syntax will look like this:

```
func variadic_function(a ...int, b int) {
    // Body of variadic function
}
```

The above `variadic_function` will fail to compile with an error syntax error:

cannot use ... with non-final parameter a

In the above function, it is not possible to pass arguments to the parameter b because whatever argument we pass will be assigned to the first parameter a since it is variadic. Hence, variadic parameters can only be present in last in the function definition. The way variadic functions work is by converting the variable number of arguments to a slice of the type of the variadic parameter. You will learn the concept of slices in *Chapter 5: Slices* in detail:

Program 2.6

```go
// Go program to explain the variadic function
package main

import (
    "fmt"
    "strings"
)


// Variadic function to join strings
func join(element ...string) string {
    return strings.Join(element, "_")
}


func main() {

    // multiple arguments
    fmt.Println(join("GO", "language", "book"))
```

```
}
```

The following will be the output for the above program:

GO_language_book

The variadic function increases the readability of your program. It can be used in scenarios such as when the number of parameters is not known.

Let's look at the following program:

Program 2.7

```
// Go program to explain the variadic function
package main

import (
    "fmt"
    "strings"
)

// Variadic function to join strings
func join(element ...string) string {
    return strings.Join(element, "_")
}

func main() {

    // pass a slice in variadic function
    element := []string{"GO", "language", "book"}
    fmt.Println(join(element...))
}
```

The following will be the output for the above program:

GO_language_book

Let's look at another program:

Program 2.8

```
//Select single argument from all arguments of variadic function
```

```
package main

import "fmt"

func main() {
    variadicExample("IT", "Finance", "HR", "Recruitement", "Payroll")
}

func variadicExample(x ...string) {
    fmt.Println(x[1])
    fmt.Println(x[4])
}
```

The following will be the output for the above program:

Finance

Payroll

2.6 Defer

Go has mechanisms for control flow: if, for, switch, goto, etc, but some of the less commonly used ones are deferred, panic, and recover.

2.6.1 Defer

A defer statement postpones the execution of a function and pushes a function call onto a list until the surrounding function returns, either normally or through a panic. Defer is commonly used to simplify functions that perform various clean-up actions as shown below:

```
Program 2.9

//Program to explain defer

package main

import "fmt"

func main() {
```

```
    defer fmt.Println("GO")
    fmt.Println("Book")
}
```

The following will be the output for the above program:

Book

GO

Conclusion

- A function declaration consists of the keyword func, the name of the function, a parameter list (empty for main), a result list, and the body of the function—the statements that define what it does—enclosed in braces.

- When a function is invoked, you pass a value to the parameter. This value is referred to as an actual parameter or argument. The parameter list refers to the type, order, and the number of the parameters of a function.

- When a program calls a function, the program control is transferred to the called function. A called function performs a defined task, and when its return statement is executed or when its function-ending closing brace is reached, it returns the program control to the main program.

- In Go, a function can return multiple values using the return statement. The type of return values depends on the type of the parameters defined in the parameter list.

- Golang allows giving names to the return parameters of the functions in the function definition, i.e., explicit naming of return variables in the function definition. It eliminates the need to mention the variable's name with the return statement.

- Go does not have a call by reference since it doesn't have reference variables. However, we can pass the address of the variable as a value. Here, we will use the concept of pointers and dereference operators. The address operator, & is used to get the address of a variable of any data type and the dereference operator, * is used to access the value at an address.

- Functions, in general, accept only a fixed number of arguments but the variadic function can accept a variable number of arguments. Only the last parameter of a function can be variadic. If the last parameter of a function definition is prefixed by an ellipsis, . . ., then the function can accept any number of arguments for that parameter.

- The variadic function increases the readability of your program. It can be used in the scenarios when the number of parameters is not known.

- A `defer` statement postpones the execution of a function and pushes a function call onto a list until the surrounding function returns, either normally or through a panic. Defer is commonly used to simplify functions that perform various clean-up actions.

Questions

1. Write the syntax for creating a function in Golang.
2. What is the difference between multiple returns and named returns? Explain with a Go program.
3. Write a Go program to explain call by value in Golang.
4. What are variadic functions? Explain scenarios where it can be used.
5. What is the `defer` statement in Golang?

CHAPTER 3
Control flows

In Go, the control flow statements are used to break the flow of execution and enable programs to execute code based on certain conditions. This chapter will cover the concept of control flows in Go. It will cover decision-making in Golang using `if`, `if...else`, `if...else if...else`, `switch...case` and `fallthrough` statements. It will also cover the concept of loops - `for` loops, nested `for` loops, loop control statements – `break`, `goto`, `continue`, etc.

Structure

- Decision making (if, if...else, if...else if...else, switch...case)
- Loops (for loops, nested for loops, loop control statements- break, goto, continue, infinite loop) and fallthrough
- Programming examples

Objective

The objective of this chapter is to introduce the concepts of control flows and loops to the readers and cover how to use them in the Go programming language.

3.1 Decision-making

Golang uses control statements to control the execution flow of the program based on certain conditions. These are used to ensure a logical flow during program execution based on changes to the state of a program.

3.1.1 If statement

A statement executes a piece of code if one condition is found true. If the statement looks as it does in C or Java, there is just one difference which is that we need to use { } instead of ( ). The variables declared by the statement are only in scope until the end of the if.

Syntax:

```
If condition {
    // piece of code to be executed when the condition is true
}
```

For example, the program given below will print if the variable a is true.

```
Program 3.1
```

```
// Go program to explain if statement

package main

import (
    "fmt"
)

func main() {
    var x = "Cricket"
    a := true
    if a {
        fmt.Println(x)
    }
}
```

The following will be the output for the above program:

`Cricket`

3.1.2 if...else statement

If the statement executes a block of statements when the condition is true, and `if` the condition is false, it will move to the `else` block and execute it.

Syntax:

```
If condition {
    // piece of code to be executed if condition is true
} else {
    // piece of code to be executed if condition is false
}
```

The following example will show the output `Capital of India` if the x is `New Delhi`:

```
Program 3.2
// Go program to explain if ...else statement

package main

import (
    "fmt"
)

func main() {
    x := "New Delhi"

    if x == "New Delhi" {
        fmt.Println("Capital of India")
    } else {
        fmt.Println("City is not the capital of India")
    }
}
```

The following will be the output for the above program:

```
Capital of India
```

3.1.3 if...else if...else statement

The if...else if...else statement allows for combining multiple if...else statements.

Syntax:

```
if condition-1 {
    // piece of code to be executed if condition-1 is true
} else if condition-2 {
    // piece of code to be executed if condition-2 is true
} else {
    // piece code to be executed if both condition1 and condition2 are
        false
}
```

The example given below will show the following output:

"Capital of Maharashtra" if x is "Mumbai"

"City of Maharashtra" if x is "Pune" and

"Neither Pune nor Mumbai" if x is other than "Pune" or "Mumbai"

Let's look at the following example:

```
Program 3.3
// Go program to explain if …else if..else statement
package main

import (
    "fmt"
)

func main() {
    x := "Mumbai"

    if x == "Mumbai" {
```

```
        fmt.Println("Capital of Maharashtra")
    } else if x == "Pune" {
        fmt.Println("City of Maharshtra")
    } else {
        fmt.Println("Neither Pune nor Mumbai")
    }
}
```

The above program will show the following output:

```
Capital of Maharashtra
```

3.1.4 switch...case

A switch statement is a multiway branch statement. It provides an efficient way of transfering the execution to different parts of a code based on the value of the expression. Switch statements express conditionals across many branches. The cases are evaluated from top to bottom, stopping when a case succeeds. If no case matches and there is a default case, its statements are executed.

The example given below will display the day of the week based on the value of a switch variable:

Program 3.4

```
// Go program to explain switch…case statement

package main

import "fmt"

func main() {
    switch day := 7; day {
        case 1:
            fmt.Println("Monday")
        case 2:
            fmt.Println("Tuesday")
        case 3:
            fmt.Println("Wednesday")
```

```
        case 4:
            fmt.Println("Thursday")
        case 5:
            fmt.Println("Friday")
        case 6:
            fmt.Println("Saturday")
        case 7:
            fmt.Println("Sunday")
        default:
            fmt.Println("Invalid")
    }


}
```

The above program will show below output:

```
Sunday
```

3.2 Loops

A loop statement is used to execute a block of code repeatedly. For is the only loop available in Go. Go doesn't have `while` or `do...while` loops that are present in other languages like C.

3.2.1 For loops

The `for` loop is a repetition control structure. It allows you to write a loop that needs to be executed a specific number of times.

Syntax:

```
for [ Initial Statement ] ; [ Condition ] ; [ Post Statement ] {
    [Action]
}
```

The example given below will display the sum of the numbers from 1 to 10 using for loop:

```
Program 3.5
```

```
// Go program to explain for loops
```

```
package main

import "fmt"

func main() {
    sum := 0
    for i := 0; i <= 10; i++ {
        sum += i
    }
    fmt.Println("Sum of numbers from 1 to 10:", sum)
}
```

The above program will show the following output:

```
Sum of numbers from 1 to 10: 55
```

3.2.2 Nested for loops

Loops can be nested in Go as they can with other programming languages. A nested loop is a loop that occurs within another loop. These can be useful when you want a looped action performed on every element of a data set.

```
for {
    [Action to be performed]
    for {
        [Action to be performed]
    }
}
```

The example given below will display the prime number from 1 to 20 using nested for loop:

```
Program 3.6
// Go program to explain nested for loops

package main
```

```go
import "fmt"

func main() {
    /* local variable declaration */
    var i, j int

    for i = 2; i < 20; i++ {
        for j = 2; j <= (i / j); j++ {
            if i%j == 0 {
                break
            }
        }
        if j > (i / j) {
            fmt.Printf("Prime number between 1 to 20: %d\n", i)
        }
    }
}
```

The above program will show the following output:

```
Prime number between 1 to 20: 2
Prime number between 1 to 20: 3
Prime number between 1 to 20: 5
Prime number between 1 to 20: 7
Prime number between 1 to 20: 11
Prime number between 1 to 20: 13
Prime number between 1 to 20: 17
Prime number between 1 to 20: 19
```

3.2.3 Loop control statements

Loop control statements are used to change the execution of the program. When the execution of the given loop leaves its scope, the objects that are created within the scope are also destroyed.

Go language supports 3 types of loop control statements: break, goto, and continue.

3.2.3.1 Break statements

A break statement is used to terminate the loop or statement in which it presents. The break statement is used to terminate the execution of the current loop.

The example given below gives the output numbers starting from 1 and at x=4, break is encountered and it goes out of the loop:

Program 3.7

```go
// Go program to explain break statements


package main


import "fmt"


// Main function
func main() {
    for x := 1; x <= 5; x++ {

        fmt.Println("Number:", x)

        // For loop breaks when the value of x = 4
        if x == 4 {
            break
        }
    }


}
```

The above program will show the following output:

```
Number: 1
Number: 2
Number: 3
Number: 4
```

3.2.3.2 Goto statements

The Goto statement is used to transfer control to the labeled statement in the program. The label is a valid identifier and placed just before the statement from where the control is transferred.

The example given below shows output numbers starting from 1 and at a=3, goto is encountered and without printing 3, control moves to Lable1.

Program 3.8

```go
// Go program to explain Goto statement

package main

import "fmt"

func main() {
    var a int = 1

Lable1:
    for a <= 5 {
        if a == 3 {
            a = a + 1
                goto Lable1
        }
        fmt.Printf("Number is: %d\n", a)
        a++

    }
}
```

The above program will show the following output:

```
Number is: 1
Number is: 2
Number is: 4
Number is: 5
```

3.2.3.3 Continue statements

The continue statement is used to skip over the execution part of the loop on a certain condition. After that, it transfers the control to the beginning of the loop.

The continue statement is used when you want to skip the remaining portion of the loop and return to the top of the loop and continue a new iteration. The example given below shows output numbers starting from 1 and at a=7, the continue statement is encountered and without printing the number 7, the control moves to the top of the loop for the next iteration.

Program 3.9

```
// Go program to explain Continue statement


package main


import "fmt"


func main() {
    var a int = 1

    for a <= 10 {
        if a == 7 {
            // skip one iteration
            a++
            continue
        }
        fmt.Printf("Number is: %d\n", a)
        a++
    }
}
```

The above program will show the following output:

```
Number is: 1
Number is: 2
Number is: 3
```

```
Number is: 4
Number is: 5
Number is: 6
Number is: 8
Number is: 9
Number is: 10
```

3.2.3.4 Infinite loop

In Go, a for loop can work as an infinite loop if you omit the loop condition or use a true boolean. The example given below keeps on printingthe Infinite Loop forever:

Program 3.10

```go
// Go program to explain Infinite loop


package main

import (
    "fmt"
    "time"
)


func main() {
    for true {
        fmt.Println("Infinite Loop")
        time.Sleep(time.Second)
    }
}
```

The above program will show the following output:

```
Infinite Loop
Infinite Loop
Infinite Loop
Infinite Loop
Infinite Loop
```

.... •

.... •

3.2.3.5 Fallthrough

In Go, the program control comes out of the switch statement just after a case is executed. But by using the Fallthrough statement, control can be transferred to the first statement of the next case clause in an expression "switch" statement.

Program 3.11

```
// Go program to explain fallthrough


package main


import (
    "fmt"
)


func main() {
    switch number := 200; {
    case number < 300:
        fmt.Printf("%d is less than 300\n", number)
        fallthrough
    case number > 100:
        fmt.Printf("%d is greater than 100", number)
    }
}
```

The above program will show the following output:

200 is less than 300

200 is greater than 100

Fallthrough cannot be used in the last case of a switch since there are no more cases present. If Fallthrough is used in the last case, it will give the following compilation error:

cannot fallthrough final case in switch

Program 3.12

```go
// Go program using fallthrough in last case

package main

import (
    "fmt"
)

func number() int {
    sum := 10 + 20
    return sum
}

func main() {

    switch sum := number(); {
    case sum < 40:
        fmt.Printf("%d is lesser than 40\n", sum)
        fallthrough
    case sum > 20:
        fmt.Printf("%d is greater than 20", sum)
        fallthrough
    }
}
```

The above program will show the following output:

cannot fallthrough final case in switch

Conclusion

- The control statements in Golang are used to control the execution flow of a given program based on certain conditions. These are used to ensure logical flow during program execution based on the changes in the state of a program.

- In `if...else` statement, the if statement will execute a block of statements when the condition is found true; and if the condition is false, it will move to the else block and execute it.

- The `if...else if...else` statement allows combining multiple `if...else` statements.

- The switch statement is a multiway branch statement and provides an efficient way to transfer the execution to different parts of the code based on the value of the expressions. The cases are evaluated from top to bottom and stop when a case is found true. If no case matches and there is a default case present, then it gets executed.

- A loop statement is used to execute a given block of code repeatedly. `For` is the only loop available in the Go language. Unlike C, Go doesn't support a `while` or `do...while` loops.

- A nested loop is a loop that occurs within another loop and these are useful when looped action needs to be performed on every element of a data set. Loops can be nested in Go as they can with other programming languages.

- When the execution of a given loop leaves its scope, the objects created within that scope are also destroyed. Loop control statements are used to change the execution of the program.

- A `break` statement is used to terminate the current loop or statement in which it presents.

- The `goto` statement is used to transfer control to the labeled statement in the Go program. The label is a valid identifier and placed just before the statement from where the control is transferred.

- The `continue` statement is used to skip over the execution part of a given loop on a certain condition. And after that, it transfers the control to the beginning of the loop.

- In Go language, a `for` loop can work as an infinite loop if you omit the loop condition or use a true Boolean.

- In Golang, the program control comes out of the switch statement just after a case is executed. But by using the `fallthrough` statement, control can be transferred to the first statement of the next case clause in an expression "switch" statement.

Questions

1. Write a Go program to explain the use of `if..else` statement.
2. State true or false:
    a. The `for` loop is not available in Golang.
    b. Go doesn't have `while` or do...while loops .
    c. The `for` loop is available in Golang.
3. Write the syntax of `if...else if...else` statement.
4. What is the `switch...case` statement? Write a Go program to explain the use of the `switch...case` statement.
5. What is the role of the `goto` statement in the Go program? Explain with a Go program.
6. How many types of loop control statements does Go support? Write a Go program to explain it.
7. State true or false:
    a. The `goto` statement is used to transfer control to the labeled statement in the Go program.
    b. The `continue` statement is not used to skip over the execution part of the loop on a certain condition.
    c. In Go, a `for` loop can work as an infinite loop if you omit the loop condition or use a true.
8. Write the syntax for nested `for` loops in Golang.

CHAPTER 4
Arrays

In Go, an array is a fixed-sized collection of elements of the same type. The elements of the array are stored sequentially and can be accessed using their index. When arrays are once defined in Go, they cannot be expanded to fit more data. Go is a statically typed language. Mixing different values belonging to different data types in an array is not allowed.

Structure

- Array declaration
- Array initialization
- Array literals
- Default value and array types
- Access and assign array elements
- 2D and 3D array
- Array iteration
- Passing arrays to functions
- Programming examples

Objective

The objective of this chapter is to introduce the concepts of array to the readers. It also covers declaring, initializing, and passing arrays to function in the Go programming language.

4.1 Arrays

An array is a sort of container that holds values of the same type. Arrays in Go have fixed length; and once they are defined, they cannot be expanded to fit more data. However, this problem can be solved using slices about which you will learn in the next chapter.

An array is a fixed-length sequence that is used to store homogeneous elements in the memory. In Go, like many other languages, arrays are fixed. Declaring an array requires that we specify the size. Once the size is specified, it cannot grow. An array is a numbered sequence of elements of a single type with a fixed length.

The elements of an array are indexed by using the [ ] index operator with their zero-based position, which means that the index of the first element is `array[0]` and the index of the last element is `array[len(array)-1]`.

4.2 Array declaration

In the Go language, arrays can be created in two different ways: by using var keyword or shorthand declaration. In Go, the array index starts from 0 which is the first element. Hence, the last element index is `n-1` where n is the length of the array. To access any element in the array, we need to use `a[index]` syntax where a is an array variable.

4.2.1 Using var keyword

An array is created using the var keyword of a type with the name, size, and elements.

Syntax:

```
var array_name[length]Type
```

For example, a `var team [15]int` can hold up to 15 scores using the indexes `team[0]` through `team[14]`. Attempts to access an out of range index in the array will result in a compiler or runtime error.

The following example below will print an array of size 5:

Program 4.1

```
// Go program to explain the use of var keyword


package main


import "fmt"


func main() {
    var x [5]int
    fmt.Println(x)
}
```

The following will be the output of the above code:

```
[0 0 0 0 0]
```

Since we haven't assigned any value to x, we just defined the array but not the value of the array elements. So, it will have zero value of its data type.

4.2.2 Shorthand declaration

Syntax:

```
array_name:= [length]Type{item1, item2, item3,...itemN}
```

Let's look at the following program:

Program 4.2

```
// Go program to explain use shorthand declaration


package main


import "fmt"


func main() {

    arr := [5]string{"Ganga", "Yamuna", "Godavari", "Kaveri", "Narmada"}
```

```
    fmt.Println("Array elements:")


    for i := 0; i <= 4; i++ {

        fmt.Println(arr[i])

    }


}
```

The following will be the output for the above program:

Array elements:

Ganga

Yamuna

Godavari

Kaveri

Narmada

4.3 Array initialization

If an array is not initialized explicitly, the default value array will be zero. An array can be initialized in Go with pre-defined values using an array literal.

An array literal contains the number of elements it will hold in square brackets, followed by the type of its elements. This is followed by a list of initial values separated by commas of each element inside the curly braces. There is no need to define all elements of an array.

Let's look at the following program:

```
Program 4.3

// Go program to explain array initialization


package main


import "fmt"


func main() {
```

```
    a := [5]int{2, 4, 6, 8, 10} // Initialized with values
    var b [5]int = [5]int{1, 3} // Partial assignment


    fmt.Println("Array a:", a)
    fmt.Println("Array b:", b)
}
```

The following will be the output for the above program:

Array a: [2 4 6 8 10]

Array b: [1 3 0 0 0]

When we initialize an array with ellipses(...) instead of specifying the length, the compiler identifies the length of an array based on the elements specified in the array declaration. The Go compiler will find the length on its own. You can only use this operator when you are defining an array with an initial value. Go provides a built-in function, len which is used to calculate the length of many data types. In this case, we can use it to calculate the length of the array as shown below:

Program 4.4

```
// Go program for array length


package main


import (
    "fmt"
    "reflect"
)


func main() {
    a := [...]int{5, 10, 15, 20, 25}


    fmt.Println(reflect.ValueOf(a).Kind())
    fmt.Println("Length of Array:", len(a))
}
```

The following will be the output for the above program:

array

Length of Array: 5

When an array is declared using an array literal, values can be initialized for specific array elements. Each element has an associated integer index showing its position in the array.

Program 4.5

```go
// Go program to initialize the value of specific array element


package main


import "fmt"


func main() {
    a := [5]int{0: 5, 2: 10, 4: 15}
    fmt.Println("Array a:", a)
}
```

The following will be the output for the above program:

Array a: [5 0 10 0 15]

We can set a value at an index using the array[index] = value syntax and get a value with array[index]. To access any element in the array, we need to use the a[index] syntax where a is an array variable. This is shown as follows:

Program 4.6

```go
// Go program to set the value at a particular array index and access it


package main


import "fmt"


func main() {

    var x [5]int
```

```
    fmt.Println("Empty array:", x)


    x[3] = 10 //value assigned at 3rd array index
    fmt.Println("Array x:", x)
    fmt.Println("Value assigned at 3rd array index:", x[3])
}
```

The following will be the output for the above program:

Empty array: [0 0 0 0 0]

Array x: [0 0 0 10 0]

Value assigned at 3rd array index: 10

4.4 2D and 3D array

Array types are one-dimensional but you can compose types to build multi-dimensional data structures. The array itself is a type in the Go language. An array is a collection of the same data type. For example, an array of integers or an array of strings.

```
Program 4.7
// Go program to explain the 2D array


package main


import "fmt"


func main() {

    var a [2][3]int
    for i := 0; i < 2; i++ {
        for j := 0; j < 3; j++ {
            a[i][j] = i + j
        }
    }
    fmt.Println("2D Array:", a)
```

```
}
```

The following will be the output for the above program:

2D Array: [[0 1 2] [1 2 3]]

Let's look at the following code:

```
Program 4.8
// Go program to explain 3D array

package main

import "fmt"

func main() {
    a := [3][3]string{{"Pune", "Mumbai", "Nagpur"},
        {"Lucknow", "Gorakhpur", "Varanasi"},
        {"Ahmedabad", "Vadodara", "Rajkot"}}
    fmt.Println("3D Array:", a)

}
```

The following will be the output for the above program:

3D Array: [[Pune Mumbai Nagpur] [Lucknow Gorakhpur Varanasi] [Ahmedabad Vadodara Rajkot]]

4.5 Array iteration

In Go, we can use the for loop to iterate over an array. Also, Go provides a range operator which returns the index and value of each element of an array in for loop.

```
Program 4.9
//Go program to iterate over an array

package main

import "fmt"
```

```go
func main() {
    x := [...]int{10, 20, 30, 40, 50}
    for index := 0; index < len(x); index++ {
        fmt.Printf("x[%d] = %d\n", index, x[index])
    }


}
```

The following will be the output for the above program:

x[0] = 10

x[1] = 20

x[2] = 30

x[3] = 40

x[4] = 50

Let's look at the following code:

```go
Program 4.10
//Go program to iterate over an array using range


package main


import "fmt"


func main() {
    x := [...]int{10, 20, 30, 40, 50}
    for index, value := range x {
        fmt.Printf("x[%d] = %d\n", index, value)
    }


}
```

The following will be the output for the above program:

```
x[0] = 10
x[1] = 20
```

```
x[2] = 30
x[3] = 40
x[4] = 50
```

If you are not interested in the index, we can just assign it to the blank identifier as shown below:

Program 4.11

```
//Go program to iterate over an array

package main

import "fmt"

func main() {
    x := [...]int{10, 20, 30, 40, 50}
    for _, value := range x {
        fmt.Println(value)
    }

}
```

The following will be the output for the above program:

```
10
20
30
40
50
```

4.6 Passing arrays to functions

When you pass an array to a function, they are passed by value like the int or string data type. The function receives only a copy of it. Hence, when you make changes to an array inside a function, it won't be reflected in the original array. But this is not the case with a slice which you will study in the next chapter.

In Go language, you can pass an array as an argument in the function. For passing an array as an argument in the function, you should first create a formal parameter using the following syntax.

For sized array:

```
func function_name(variable_name [size]type){

    // function body

}
```

Or, for unsized array:

```
func function_name(variable_name []type){

    // function body

}
```

In the example given below, we have a function named as arr_sum() which accepts an array as an argument. In the main function, we have passed x[5] of int type to the function along with the size of the array and the function returns the sum of the array elements.

Program 4.12

```
// Go program for passing arrays to a function
package main

import "fmt"

// This function accepts array as an argument
func arr_sum(a [5]int, size int) int {
    var i, sum int

    for i = 0; i < size; i++ {
        sum += a[i]
    }
    return sum
}


// Main function
```

```go
func main() {

    // Create and initialize array
    var x = [5]int{10, 20, 30, 40, 50}
    var sum int

    // Pass array as an argument
    sum = arr_sum(x, 5)
    fmt.Printf("Sum of array elements: %d ", sum)
}
```

The following will be the output for the above program:

Sum of array elements: 150

In the example given below, we have explained the concept of passing arrays to functions using a function named as arr_avg() which accepts an array as an argument. In the main function, we have passed x[4] of int type to the function along with the size of the array and the function returns average of the array elements as shown below:

Program 4.13

```go
// Go program for passing arrays to a function (another example)
package main

import "fmt"

// This function accepts array as an argument
func arr_avg(a [4]int, size int) int {
    var i, sum, avg int

    for i = 0; i < size; i++ {
        sum += a[i]
    }
    avg = sum / size
```

```go
    return avg
}


// Main function
func main() {

    // Create and initialize array
    var x = [4]int{20, 40, 60, 80}
    var avg int

    // Pass array as an argument
    avg = arr_avg(x, 4)
    fmt.Printf("Average of array elements: %d ", avg)
}
```

The following will be the output for the above program:

```
Average of array elements: 50
```

Conclusion

- An array is a fixed-size collection of elements of the same type in the Go language. The elements of the array are stored sequentially and can be accessed using their index.

- Arrays can be created in the Go language by either using the var keyword or shorthand declaration.

- To access any element in the array, we need to use a[index] syntax where a is an array variable. In Go, the first array element will have index 0 and the last element will have index n-1 where n is the length of the array.

- An array can be initialized in the Go language with pre-defined values using an array literal. If an array is not initialized explicitly, then the default value array is zero.

- In Go, when an array is initialized with ellipses (...) instead of specifying the length, the compiler identifies the length of an array based on the elements specified in the array declaration.

- Go provides a built-in function, len which can be used to calculate the length of an array.

- In array, we can set a value at an index using the array[index] = value syntax and get a value with array[index]. To access any element in the array, we need to use a[index] syntax where a is an array variable.

- The array itself is a type in the Go language. Array types are one-dimensional but you can compose types to build multi-dimensional data structures.

- Go is a statically typed language and hence, mixing different values belonging to different data types in an array is not allowed.

- We can use for loop to iterate over an array in the Go language. Also, Go provides a range operator which returns index and value of each element of an array in for loop.

- When you pass an array to a function, they are passed by value like an int or string data type and the function receives only a copy of it. Hence, when you make changes to an array inside a function, it won't be reflected in the original array.

Questions

1. How can we check whether or not an array is empty in Golang?
2. Write a Go program to find the length of an array.
3. Write a Go program to set the value at an array index and access it.
4. Explain the role of array in Golang. Write a Go program to iterate over an array.
5. How can we pass arrays to functions in Golang? Explain using a Go program.

CHAPTER 5
Slices

Slices are flexible and extensible data structures which can grow and shrink as per the need. Like arrays, slices are index-able and have a length. In Go, an array allows you to define variables that can hold data items of the same type but it doesn't provide any in-built method to increase its size dynamically or get a subarray, but slices overcome this limitation of arrays.

Structure

- Concept of slices
- Declaration of slice
- Creating a slice
- Modifying a slice
- Zero value slice
- Comparison of a slice
- Multi-dimensional slice
- Sorting a slice
- Iterate over a slice

Objective

The objective of this chapter is to introduce the concept of slices to the readers and show them how to declare slice, various ways to create slices, modify and compare slices, multi-dimensional slices, sorting slices, and the various ways of iterating over slices.

5.1 Concept of slices

Slice is a segment of an array that can be resized and hence, it is more flexible compared to arrays. Like arrays, slices are indexable and have a length. A slice is a lightweight structure that wraps and represents a portion of an array. Slices are created using the make function.

A slice is a variable-length sequence which stores elements of a similar type, and it's not allowed to store different types of elements in the same slice. The first index position in a slice is always 0 and the last one is (length of slice – 1).

5.2 Declaration of slice

A slice is declared just like an array but it doesn't contain the size of the slice. So, it becomes flexible and of a dynamic size to fit the requirements.

Syntax:

```
var my_slice[]int
```

For example, we have created a team with a length of 0.

```
var team []int
```

5.3 Creating a slice

A slice consists of three things – pointer, length, and capacity.

Pointer	Length	Capacity

- **Pointer**: A reference to an underlying array.
- **Length**: The length of the segment of the array that the slice contains.
- **Capacity**: The maximum size up to which the segment can grow.

5.3.1 Creating a slice using a slice literal

A slice can be created using slice literal. This is shown as follows:

```
var s = []int{2, 4, 6, 8, 10}
```

When you create a slice using a slice literal, it first creates an array and then returns a slice reference to it as shown below:

```
Program 5.1
```

```go
// Go program to create a slice using slice literal


package main


import "fmt"


func main() {
    // Create a slice using a slice literal
    var s = []int{2, 4, 6, 8, 10}

    fmt.Println("slice =", s)


}
```

The following will be the output for the above program:

slice = [2 4 6 8 10]

The following is another way to create a slice using a slice literal by shorthand declaration:

```
Program 5.2
```
```go
// Go program to create a slice


package main


import "fmt"
```

```
func main() {
    // Create a slice using a slice literal using short hand declaration
    s := []int{1, 3, 5, 7, 9}

    fmt.Println("slice =", s)

}
```

The following will be the output for the above program:

slice = [1 3 5 7 9]

5.3.2 Creating a slice from an array

To create a slice from an array, we specify two indices, lower bound and upper bound separated by a colon. Let us suppose that you have an array and you want to obtain a slice from this array.

```
array_name[low:high]
```

The above expression selects a slice from a given array. The resulting slice includes all the elements starting from the index low to high but excludes the element at index high.

Program 5.3

```
// Go program to create a slice from array

package main

import "fmt"

func main() {
    var a = [6]string{"Jaipur", "Gorakhpur", "Pune", "Bengaluru", "Mumbai",
    "Delhi"}

    // Create a slice from the array
    var s []string = a[1:5]

    fmt.Println("Array a =", a)
```

```
    fmt.Println("Slice s =", s)
}
```

The following will be the output for the above program:

```
Array a = [Jaipur Gorakhpur Pune Bengaluru Mumbai Delhi]
Slice s = [Gorakhpur Pune Bengaluru Mumbai]
```

The low and high indices in the slice expression are optional. The default value for low is 0 and high is the length of the slice.

Program 5.4

```
// Go program to create a slice from array

package main

import "fmt"

func main() {
    a := [6]string{"Pune", "Bengaluru", "Mumbai", "Delhi", "Gorakhpur",
        "Jaipur"}

    slice1 := a[:2]
    slice2 := a[3:]
    slice3 := a[:]

    fmt.Println("Array a =", a)
    fmt.Println("slice1 =", slice1)
    fmt.Println("slice2 =", slice2)
    fmt.Println("slice3 =", slice3)
}
```

The following will be the output for the above program:

```
Array a = [Pune Bengaluru Mumbai Delhi Gorakhpur Jaipur]
slice1 = [Pune Bengaluru]
slice2 = [Delhi Gorakhpur Jaipur]
slice3 = [Pune Bengaluru Mumbai Delhi Gorakhpur Jaipur]
```

5.3.3 Creating a slice from another slice

You can create a slice from an existing slice:

Program 5.5

```
// Go program to create a slice from another slice


package main


import "fmt"


func main() {
    a   :=  [8]string{"Shanghai",  "Hiroshima",  "Jaipur",  "Gorakhpur",
    "Nagpur", "Mumbai", "Nashik", "Lucknow"}

    ind_cities := a[2:]
    maha_cities := ind_cities[2:5]

    fmt.Println("Cities =", a)
    fmt.Println("Indian Cities =", ind_cities)
    fmt.Println("Maharashtra Cities =", maha_cities)
}
```

The following will be the output for the above program:

```
Cities = [Shanghai Hiroshima Jaipur Gorakhpur Nagpur Mumbai Nashik Lucknow]
Indian Cities = [Jaipur Gorakhpur Nagpur Mumbai Nashik Lucknow]
Maharashtra Cities = [Nagpur Mumbai Nashik]
```

5.3.4 Create slice using make() function

You can also create a slice using the make() function provided by the Go library. This function takes three parameters - type, length, and capacity. Here, the capacity value is optional. It assigns an underlying array with a size that is equal to the given capacity and returns a slice, which refers to the underlying array.

Program 5.6

```
// Go program to create slice using make() function
```

```
package main

import "fmt"

func main() {

    // Creating an array of size 8 and slice this array till 5
    // and return the reference of the slice using make function
    var my_slice = make([]int, 5, 8)
    fmt.Printf("Slice = %v", my_slice)
    fmt.Printf("\nLength = %d", len(my_slice))
    fmt.Printf("\nCapacity = %d", cap(my_slice))

}
```

The following will be output for the above program:

Slice = [0 0 0 0 0]
Length = 5
Capacity = 8

5.4 Modifying a Slice

Slices are reference types and they refer to an underlying array. Therefore, modifying an element of a slice will modify the corresponding elements in the referenced array, and the other slices that refer to the same array will also see those modifications.

Program 5.7

```
// Go program to modify a slice

package main

import "fmt"

func main() {
```

```
    a := [7]string{"One", "Two", "Three", "Four", "Five", "Six", "Seven"}

    slice1 := a[1:]
    slice2 := a[3:]

    fmt.Println("***** Before Modifications *****")
    fmt.Println("Array  =", a)
    fmt.Println("slice1 =", slice1)
    fmt.Println("slice2 =", slice2)

    slice1[0] = "TWO"
    slice1[2] = "FOUR"

    slice2[1] = "FIVE"

    fmt.Println("\n***** After Modifications *****")
    fmt.Println("Array  =", a)
    fmt.Println("slice1 =", slice1)
    fmt.Println("slice2 =", slice2)
}
```

The following will be the output for the above program:

```
***** Before Modifications *****
Array = [One Two Three Four Five Six Seven]
slice1 = [Two Three Four Five Six Seven]
slice2 = [Four Five Six Seven]

***** After Modifications *****
Array = [One TWO Three FOUR FIVE Six Seven]
slice1 = [TWO Three FOUR FIVE Six Seven]
slice2 = [FOUR FIVE Six Seven]
```

5.5 Zero-value slice

Nil slice does not contain any element in it. So, the capacity and the length of this slice is 0. Nil slice does not contain an array reference. Let's look at the following example:

Program 5.8

```
// Go program to create zero value slice


package main


import "fmt"


func main() {

    // Creating a zero value slice
    var my_slice []string
    fmt.Printf("Length of Slice = %d\n", len(my_slice))
    fmt.Printf("Capacity of Slice = %d ", cap(my_slice))


}
```

The following will be the output for the above program:

Length of Slice = 0
Capacity of Slice = 0

5.6 Comparison of slice

You can use the == operator in slice to check whether given slice is nil or not. Let's look at the following example:

Program 5.9

```
// Go program to check if slice is nil or not


package main
```

```go
import "fmt"

func main() {

    // creating slices
    s1 := []int{1, 2, 3, 4, 5}
    var s2 []int

    // Check if slice is nil or not
    fmt.Println(s1 == nil)
    fmt.Println(s2 == nil)
}
```

The following will be output for the above program:

false

true

5.7 Multi-dimensional Slice

The multi-dimensional slice is just like the multidimensional array, except that the slice does not contain the size. Let's look at the following example:

Program 5.10

```go
// Go program to create and access multi-dimensional slice

package main

import "fmt"

func main() {

    // Creating multi-dimensional slice
    s1 := [][]int{{10, 20},
        {40, 80},
        {50, 100},
```

```
        {200, 400},
    }


    // Accessing multi-dimensional slice
    fmt.Println("Slice 1 :", s1)


    // Creating multi-dimensional slice
    s2 := [][]string{
        []string{"Rajasthan", "Jaipur"},
        []string{"Maharashtra", "Mumbai"},
        []string{"Karnataka", "Bengaluru"},
    }


    // Accessing multi-dimensional slice
    fmt.Println("Slice 2 :", s2)


}
```

The following will be the output for the above program:

Slice 1 : [[10 20] [40 80] [50 100] [200 400]]

Slice 2 : [[Rajasthan Jaipur] [Maharashtra Mumbai] [Karnataka Bengaluru]]

5.8 Sorting of slice

In the Go language, you can sort the elements present in the slice. The standard Go library provides the sort package which contains different types of sorting methods for sorting the slices of Ints, float64s, and Strings. Let's look at the following example:

Program 5.11

```
// Go program to create slice and perform sort operation


package main


import (
```

```go
    "fmt"
    "sort"
)

func main() {

    // Creating Slice
    slice1 := []string{"India", "Japan", "China", "Russia", "Singapore"}
    slice2 := []int{200, 500, 700, 400, 800, 300, 600, 900}

    fmt.Println("***** Before sorting *****")
    fmt.Println("Slice 1:", slice1)
    fmt.Println("Slice 2:", slice2)

    // Performing sort operation on slice
    sort.Strings(slice1)
    sort.Ints(slice2)

    fmt.Println("\n***** After sorting *****")
    fmt.Println("Slice 1:", slice1)
    fmt.Println("Slice 2:", slice2)

}
```

The following will be the output for the above program:

***** Before sorting *****
Slice 1: [India Japan China Russia Singapore]
Slice 2: [200 500 700 400 800 300 600 900]

***** After sorting *****
Slice 1: [China India Japan Russia Singapore]
Slice 2: [200 300 400 500 600 700 800 900]

5.9 Iterate over a slice

You can iterate over a slice by either using `for` loop or `range` in for loop.

5.9.1 Iterate over a slice using for loop

Let's look at the following example:

Program 5.12

```
// Go program to iterate over slice using for loop

package main

import "fmt"

func main() {

    // Creating a slice
    my_slice := []string{"Golang", "program",
        "to", "iterate", "over", "slice", "using", "for", "loop"}

    // Iterate using for loop
    for i := 0; i < len(my_slice); i++ {
        fmt.Println(my_slice[i])
    }
}
```

The following will be the output for the above program:

```
Golang
program
to
iterate
over
slice
using
```

```
for
```

```
loop
```

5.9.2 Iterate over a slice using a range in for loop

You can iterate over a slice using a range in the for a loop. By using a range in the for loop, you can also get the index and the element value. Let's look at the following program:

Program 5.13

```
// Go program to iterate over slice using a range in for loop


package main


import "fmt"


func main() {


    // Creating a slice
    my_slice := []string{"Golang", "program", "to", "iterate",
        "over", "slice", "using", "range", "in", "for", "loop"}


    // Iterate slice using range in for loop
    for index, element := range my_slice {
        fmt.Printf("Index = %d and Element = %s\n", index, element)
    }
}
```

The following will be the output for the above program:

```
Index = 0 and Element = Golang
Index = 1 and Element = program
Index = 2 and Element = to
Index = 3 and Element = iterate
Index = 4 and Element = over
Index = 5 and Element = slice
```

```
Index = 6 and Element = using
Index = 7 and Element = range
Index = 8 and Element = in
Index = 9 and Element = for
Index = 10 and Element = loop
```

Conclusion

- In Go, the slice is a segment of an array that can be resized and is more flexible compared to arrays. Like arrays, slices are indexable and have length.

- A slice is a lightweight structure that wraps and represents a portion of an array. A slice consists of three things – pointer, length, and capacity.

- In the Go language, a slice is declared just like an array but it doesn't contain the size of the slice. Therefore, it becomes flexible and dynamic in size to fit the requirements.

- In order to create a slice from an array, we specify two indices, lower bound and upper bound separated by a colon. The default value for low is 0 and high is the length of the slice. The low and high indices in the slice expression are optional.

- In Go, you can create a slice using the make() function provided by the Go library. This function takes three parameters- type, length, and capacity. Here, the capacity value is optional. It assigns an underlying array with a size that is equal to the given capacity and returns a slice which refers to the underlying array.

- The slices are reference types in the Go language and they refer to an underlying array. Hence, modifying an element of a slice will modify the corresponding elements in the referenced array and the other slices that refer to the same array will also see those modifications.

- In Go, a nil slice does not contain any element in it. So, the capacity and length of this slice are 0 and the nil slice does not contain an array reference. Also, you can use the == operator in slice to check whether a given slice is nil or not.

- In Go, the multi-dimensional slice is just like the multi-dimensional array, except that the slice does not contain the size.

- You can iterate over the slice either by using for loop or range in for loop. By using a range in the for loop, you can also get the index and the element value.

- In Go, you can sort the elements present in a slice. The standard Go library provides the sort package which contains different types of sorting methods for sorting the slices of Ints, float64s, Strings, etc.

Questions

1. How can we create a slice using slice literal? Explain using a Go program.
2. Write a Go program to create a slice from an array.
3. How can we create a slice from another slice? Explain using a Go program.
4. Write a Go program to create a slice using the make() function.
5. Write a Go program to modify a slice.
6. How can we compare two slices in Golang? Write a Go program.
7. Write a Go program to create and access the multi-dimensional slice.
8. Write a Go program to sort a slice using the sort package.
9. How can we iterate over slice? Explain using a Go program.
10. Explain different ways to iterate over the slice in Golang.

CHAPTER 6
Maps

A Golang map is a collection of unordered key-value pairs. It provides fast lookups, and we can retrieve, update, or delete values with the help of keys. Given a key and a value pair, you can store the value in a `map` object. After the value is stored, you can call the values of a map by referencing the related keys.

Structure

- What are Go maps?
- Declaration of Go maps
- Initialization of Go maps
- Iterating over Go maps
- Adding key-value pairs in maps
- Updating key-value pairs in maps
- Retrieving the value of a key in maps
- Checking if a key exists in Go Maps
- Deletion of a key from maps
- Maps are reference types

Objective

This chapter explains the basic concept of map and how to use it in the Go programming language. It covers how to declare and initialize a map, how to iterate over a map, how to retrieve, update and delete over a map, and how to check if a key exists in a map.

6.1 What are Go maps?

A map is an unordered collection of key-value pairs. The keys are unique within a map but the values may not be. It is widely used because it provides fast lookups and values that can retrieved, updated, or deleted with the help of keys.

A map is also known as an associative array, a hash table, or a dictionary. Maps are used to look up a value by its associated key.

6.2 Declaration of Go maps

A map is declared using the following syntax:

```
var m map[key_type]value_type
```

For example, you can declare a map of string keys to int values as shown below:

```
var m map[string]int
```

The zero value of a map is nil. A nil map has no keys. Therefore, any attempt to add keys to a nil map will result in a runtime error. Let's look at the following example:

Program 6.1

```
// Go program to explain the declaration of a map


package main


import "fmt"


func main() {
    var m1 map[string]int
    fmt.Println(m1)
    if m1 == nil {
        fmt.Println("Map is empty")
```

```
    } else {

        fmt.Println("Map is not empty")

    }


    // Attempt to add keys to a nil map will throw runtime error
    //m1["ten"] = 10
}
```

The following will be the output for the above code:

map[]

Map is empty

If you uncomment the statement m1["ten"] = 10, the program will give a run time error. Therefore, it is necessary to initialize a map before adding items to it.

6.3 Initialization of Go Maps

A map can be initialized by either using a map literal or the built-in make() function.

6.3.1 Initializing maps using map literal

A map literal is the easiest way to initialize a map with some data. You just need to pass the key-value pairs separated by a colon inside curly braces, and the last trailing comma is necessary as otherwise, you'll get a compiler error.

Program 6.2

```
// Go program to initialize a map using map literal
package main

import "fmt"

func main() {
    var m1 = map[string]int{
        "a": 10,
        "b": 20,
        "c": 30,
```

```
        "d": 40,
        "e": 50,
    }


    fmt.Println(m1)
}
```

The following will be the output for the above code:

map[a:10 b:20 c:30 d:40 e:50]

You can also create an empty map using a map literal by leaving the curly braces empty.

6.3.2 Initializing a map using make() function

You can initialize a map using the built-in make() function. You just need to pass the type of the map to the make() function, and it will return an initialized and ready-to-use the map. Let's look at the following program:

Program 6.3

```
// Go program to initialize a map using make() function


var m = make(map[string]int)


package main


import "fmt"


func main() {
    var m1 = make(map[string]int)
    fmt.Println(m1)
    if m1 == nil {
        fmt.Println("Map is empty")
    } else {


        fmt.Println("Map is not empty")
```

```
    }

    // make() function returns an initialized and ready to use map
    // you can add new keys
    m1["ten"] = 10
    fmt.Println(m1)
}
```

The following will be the output for the above code:

map[]

Map is not empty

map[ten:10]

6.4 Iterating over Go maps

You can iterate over a map using a range form of the for loop. It gives you the key and value pair in every iteration. Let's look at the following program:

```
Program 6.4
// Go program to explain iteration over a map
package main

import "fmt"

func main() {
    var my_map = map[string]string{
        "Maharashtra":    "Mumbai",
        "Uttar_Pradesh": "Lucknow",
        "Rajasthan":     "Jaipur",
        "Karnataka":     "Bengaluru",
    }

    for state, capital := range my_map {
        fmt.Println(state, capital)
    }
```

```
}
```

The following will be the output for the above code:

```
Maharashtra Mumbai

Uttar_Pradesh Lucknow

Rajasthan Jaipur

Karnataka Bengaluru
```

Let's look at the following example:

```
Program 6.5

// Go program to explain iteration over a map

package main

import "fmt"

func main() {
    var my_map = map[string]int{
        "India":     1947,
        "Singapore": 1965,
        "Australia": 1901,
        "Malaysia":  1957,
    }

    for country, year_of_independence := range my_map {
        fmt.Println(country, year_of_independence)
    }

}
```

The following will be the output for the above code:

India 1947

Singapore 1965

```
Australia 1901
```

```
Malaysia 1957
```

A map is an unordered collection and therefore, the iteration order of a map is not guaranteed to be the same every time that you iterate over it. So, if you run the above program multiple times, you'll get the results in different orders.

6.5 Adding key-value pairs in maps

In maps, you can add key-value pairs in the initialized map using the following syntax:

```
map_name[key]=value
```

Let's look at the following example:

Program 6.6

```go
// Go program to add key-value pairs in a map
package main

import "fmt"

func main() {

    // Create and initialize a map
    var my_map = map[int]string{
        1:   "US",
        91:  "India",
        86:  "China",
        44:  "UK",
    }

    fmt.Println("Original Map\n", my_map)

    // Adding new key-value pairs in the map
    my_map[39] = "Italy"
    my_map[81] = "Japan"
```

```
    fmt.Println("\nMap after adding new key-value pairs \n", my_map)



}
```

The following will be the output for the above code:

Original Map

 `map[1:US 44:UK 86:China 91:India]`

Map after adding new key-value pairs

 `map[1:US 39:Italy 44:UK 81:Japan 86:China 91:India]`

6.6 Updating key-value pairs in maps

In a map, if you try to add an already existing key, it will merely override or update the value of that key with the new value. Let's look at the following program:

Program 6.7

```go
// Go program to update key-value pairs in a map


package main


import "fmt"


func main() {


    // Create and initialize a map
    var my_map = map[int]string{
        1:   "US",
        91:  "India",
        86:  "China",
        44:  "UK",
    }


    fmt.Println("Original Map\n", my_map)
```

```
    // Updating values of the map
    my_map[1] = "United States"
    my_map[44] = "United Kingdom"
    fmt.Println("\nAfter updating values of the map \n", my_map)
}
```

The following will be the output for the above code:

```
Original Map
 map[1:US 44:UK 86:China 91:India]


After updating values of the map
 map[1:United States 44:United Kingdom 86:China 91:India]
```

6.7 Retrieving the value of a key in maps

In maps, you can retrieve a value with the help of keys using the following syntax:

```
map_name[key]
```

If a key doesn't exist in the given map, it will return a zero value, i.e., nil; and if the key exists in the given map, it will return the value related to that key.

```
Program 6.8
// Go program to retrieve the value of a key in a map

package main

import "fmt"

func main() {

    // Create and initialize a map
    var my_map = map[int]string{
        1:   "US",
        91:  "India",
        86:  "China",
        44:  "UK",
    }
```

```
    fmt.Println("Original Map:", my_map)

    // Retrieve values with the help of keys
    v1 := my_map[91]
    v2 := my_map[93]
    v3 := my_map[44]
    fmt.Println("Value of key[91]:", v1)
    fmt.Println("Value of key[93]:", v2)
    fmt.Println("Value of key[44]:", v3)
}
```

The following will be the output for the above code:

Original Map: map[1:US 44:UK 86:China 91:India]

Value of key[91]: India

Value of key[93]:

Value of key[44]: UK

6.8 Checking if a key exists in Go maps

When you retrieve the value assigned to a given key using the syntax map[key], it returns an additional Boolean value as well which is true if the key exists in the map and false if it doesn't exist.

You can check for the existence of a key in a map by using the following two-value assignment:

```
value, variable_name := map_name[key]
```

The Boolean variable will be true if the key exists and false otherwise.

Program 6.9

```
// Go program to check if a key exists in a map

package main

import "fmt"
```

```go
func main() {

    // Create and initialize a map
    var my_map = map[int]string{
        1:  "US",
        91: "India",
        86: "China",
        44: "UK",
    }

    fmt.Println("Original Map:", my_map)

    // Checking key is available or not in map
    country, x := my_map[91]
    fmt.Println("\nKey present or not:", x)
    fmt.Println("Value:", country)
}
```

The following will be the output for the above code:

Original Map: map[1:US 44:UK 86:China 91:India]

Key present or not: true

Value: India

If you just want to check for the existence of a key without retrieving the value associated with that key, then you can use an _ (underscore) in the place of the first value.

```
_, variable_name := map_name[key]
```

Let's look at the following example:

```
Program 6.10
// Go program to check if a key exists in a map


package main
```

```
import "fmt"

func main() {

    // Create and initialize a map
    var my_map = map[int]string{
        1:   "US",
        91: "India",
        86: "China",
        44: "UK",
    }


    fmt.Println("Original Map:", my_map)


    // Using blank identifier
    _, x := my_map[91]
    _, y := my_map[95]
    fmt.Println("\nKey 91 present or not:", x)
    fmt.Println("Key 95 present or not:", y)
}
```

The following will be the output for the above code:

```
Original Map: map[1:US 44:UK 86:China 91:India]


Key 91 present or not: true
Key 95 present or not: false
```

6.9 Deletion of a key from maps

In maps, you are allowed to delete the key present in the map using the `delete()` function. It's a built-in function. It does not return any value and doesn't perform any action if the key is not present in the given map:

```
delete(map_name, key)
```

Let's look at the following example:

Program 6.11

```go
// Go program to explain key deletion from a map
package main

import "fmt"

func main() {

    // Create and initialize a map
    var my_map = map[int]string{
        1:  "US",
        91: "India",
        86: "China",
        44: "UK",
    }

    fmt.Println("Map before deletion:\n", my_map)

    // Delete keys in a Map using delete()
    delete(my_map, 1)
    delete(my_map, 44)
    fmt.Println("\nMap after deletion:\n", my_map)
}
```

The following will be the output for the above code:

```
Map before deletion:
 map[1:US 44:UK 86:China 91:India]

Map after deletion:
 map[86:China 91:India]
```

6.10 Maps are reference types

Maps are reference types. When you assign a map to a new variable, both of them refer to the same underlying data structure. Therefore, changes done by one variable are visible to the other. Let's look at the following example:

Program 6.12

```
// Go program to explain modification concept in map
package main

import "fmt"

func main() {

    // Create and initialize a map
    var my_map = map[int]string{
        1:    "US",
        44:   "UK",
        81:   "Japan",
        91:   "India",
        972:  "Israel",
    }

    fmt.Println("Original Map:\n", my_map)

    // Assigned the map into a new variable
    new_map := my_map

    // Perform modification in new_map
    new_map[86] = "China"
    new_map[33] = "France"

    // Display map after modification
    fmt.Println("New map:\n", new_map)
```

```
    fmt.Println("Modification in old map:\n", my_map)
}
```

The following will be the output for the above code:

```
Original Map:
 map[1:US 44:UK 81:Japan 91:India 972:Israel]
New map:
 map[1:US 33:France 44:UK 81:Japan 86:China 91:India 972:Israel]
Modification in old map:
 map[1:US 33:France 44:UK 81:Japan 86:China 91:India 972:Israel]
```

Conclusion

- A map is an unordered collection of key-value pairs in Golang. The keys are unique within a map but the values may not be. It is widely used because it provides fast lookups and values that can be retrieved, updated, or deleted with the help of keys.

- In Golang, a map is also known as an associative array, a hash table, or a dictionary. A map is used to look up a value by its associated key.

- The zero value of a map is nil and a nil map has no keys. Therefore, any attempt to add keys to a nil map will result in a runtime error.

- In Go, a map can be initialized by either using a map literal or a built-in make() function.

- A map literal is the easiest way to initialize a map with some data in Go programming. You just need to pass the key-value pairs separated by a colon inside curly braces. The last trailing comma is necessary as otherwise, you'll get a compiler error.

- In Go, you can initialize a map using the built-in make() function. You just need to pass the type of the map to the make() function and it will return an initialized and ready-to-use the map.

- You can iterate over a map using a range form of the for loop in the Go programming language. It gives you the key and value pair in every iteration.

- In Golang, a map is an unordered collection and therefore, the iteration order of a map is not guaranteed to be the same every time that you iterate over it. So, if you run any program multiple times, you'll get the results in different orders.

- In a map, if you try to add an already existing key, it will merely override or update the value of that key with the new value.

- If a key doesn't exist in the given map, it will return a zero value, i.e., nil; and if the key exists in the given map, it will return the value related to that key.

- In Go, when you retrieve the value assigned to a given key using the syntax map[key], it returns an additional Boolean value as well which is true if the key exists in the map and is false if it doesn't exist.

- In maps, you are allowed to delete the key present in the map using the delete() function. It's a built-in function in Golang. It does not return any value and doesn't perform any action if the key is not present in the given map.

- Maps are reference types in Golang. When you assign a map to a new variable, both of them refer to the same underlying data structure. Therefore, changes done by one variable are visible to the other.

Questions

1. What are Golang maps? Write a Go program to initialize a map using map literal.

2. Explain the initialization of maps using the make() function in Golang.

3. Write a Go program to explain iteration over maps.

4. How can we add key-value pairs in a Golang map? Explain using a Go program.

5. Write a Go program to update key-value pairs in a Golang map.

6. How can we retrieve the value of a key in the map? Explain with the help of a Go program.

7. How can we check if a key exists in a Golang map? Write a Go program to explain it.

8. Write a Go program to explain key deletion from maps.

CHAPTER 7
Structs

A struct is a user-defined type that represents a collection of fields. A structure has different fields of the same or different data types. A struct or structure can be compared with the class in the object-oriented programming paradigm. A structure is mainly used when you need to define a schema made of different individual fields or properties.

Structure

- What are structs?
- Declaring and initializing structs type
- Zero value of structs
- Access fields of structs
- Pointer to structs
- Updating value of struct member using pointer
- Exported vs. unexported structs and struct fields
- Structs are value types
- Struct equality

Objective

This chapter explains the basic concept of a struct and how to use it in the Go programming language. It covers how to declare and initialize structs type, access fields of structs, pointer to structs, exported and unexported structs, and structs fields.

7.1 What are structs?

Structs are user-defined types that contains a collection of named fields and properties. A struct uses group related data to form a single unit. Golang can declare and create their data types by combining one or more types,including both built-in and user-defined types.

Structs are the only way to create concrete user-defined types in Golang. They improve modularity and allow them to create and pass complex data structures around the system.

7.2 Declaring and initializing structs type

The declaration of struct starts with the keyword type, then a name for the new struct, and finally, the keyword `struct`. Within the curly brackets, a series of data fields are specified with a name and their types.

You can initialize a variable of a `struct` type using a struct literal. You also need to pass the field values in the same order in which they are declared in the struct.

Syntax of structs:

```
type identifier struct{
    field_1 data_type
    field_2 data_type
}
```

Let's look at the following program:

```
Program 7.1
// Golang program to declare and define struct
package main

import "fmt"
```

```go
// Define a struct type
type city_list struct {
    city       string
    state      string
    country    string
}

func main() {

    // Declare and initialize struct using a struct literal
    c1 := city_list{"Mumbai", "Maharashtra", "India"}
    c2 := city_list{"Chicago", "Illinois", "US"}
    c3 := city_list{"Sydney", "New South Wales", "Australia"}

    fmt.Println("City1:", c1)
    fmt.Println("City2:", c2)
    fmt.Println("City3:", c3)
}
```

The following will be the output for the above code:

City1: {Mumbai Maharashtra India}

City2: {Chicago Illinois US}

City3: {Sydney New South Wales Australia}

Let's look at the following program:

```go
Program 7.2
// Golang program to declare and define struct
package main

import "fmt"

// Define a struct type
type city_list struct {
```

```go
        city     string
        state    string
        country string
}

func main() {

        // Naming fields while initializing a struct
        c1 := city_list{city: "Mumbai", state: "Maharashtra", country: "India"}
        c2 := city_list{city: "Chicago", state: "Illinois", country: "US"}
        c3 := city_list{city: "Sydney", state: "New South Wales", country:
            "Australia"}

        fmt.Println("City1:", c1)
        fmt.Println("City2:", c2)
        fmt.Println("City3:", c3)
}
```

The following will be the output for the above code:

City1: {Mumbai Maharashtra India}

City2: {Chicago Illinois US}

City3: {Sydney New South Wales Australia}

7.3 Zero value of structs

When a struct is defined, it is not explicitly initialized with any value. The fields of the struct are assigned their zero values by default.

Program 7.3

```go
// Golang program to explain zero value of a struct
package main

import (
    "fmt"
)
```

```
type employee struct {
    name string
    age int
    city string
}


func main() {
    var emp1 employee //zero valued struct
    fmt.Println("Employee1 details:", emp1)
}
```

The following will be the output for the above code:

Employee1 details: { 0 }

The above program defines emp1 but it is not initialized with any value. Hence, the name and city are assigned the zero values of string, which is "" and age is assigned the zero values of int, which is 0. Therefore, the program outputs the following:

Employee1 details: { 0 }

It is also possible to specify values for some fields and ignore the rest of the fields. In this case, the ignored field names are assigned zero values. Let's look at the following program:

```
Program 7.4
// Golang program to explain zero value of a struct
package main


import (
    "fmt"
)


type employee struct {
    name     string
    age      int
    location string
```

```
}

func main() {
    emp1 := employee{
        age:    30,
        location: "Pune",
    }
    fmt.Println("Employee1 details:", emp1)
}
```

The following will be the output for the above code:

Employee1 details: { 30 Pune}

7.4 Access fields of structs

To access the individual fields of a struct, you must use the dot (.) operator:

Program 7.5

```
// Golang program to access fields of struct
package main

import "fmt"

// define struct
type bike struct {
    name, model, color string
    weight_in_kg     float64
}

// Main Function
func main() {
    b := bike{name: "Bajaj", model: "Pulsar_150cc",
        color: "Black Grey", weight_in_kg: 148}

    // Access struct fields using the dot operator
```

```
    fmt.Println("bike name:", b.name)
    fmt.Println("bike color:", b.color)


    // Assign a new value to a struct field
    b.color = "Neon Red"


    // Display result
    fmt.Println("bike:", b)
}
```

The following will be the output for the above code:

bike name: Bajaj

bike color: Black Grey

bike: {Bajaj Pulsar_150cc Neon Red 148}

7.5 Pointer to structs

Pointer in Golang is a variable which is used to store the memory address of another variable. The variables are used to store some data at a memory address in the system.

You can also use a pointer to a struct with the help of the & operator, i.e., the address operator. Golang allows programmers to access the fields of a structure using the pointers without any dereferencing explicitly. Let's look at the following program:

```
Program 7.6
// Golang program to explain the concept of the pointer in the struct
package main


import "fmt"


type my_struct struct {
    city    string
    country string
}
```

```go
func main() {

    // create instance of my_struct
    my_struct1 := my_struct{"New Delhi", "India"}

    // pointer to the struct
    my_pointer := &my_struct1

    fmt.Println(my_pointer)

    // accessing struct field using a pointer
    fmt.Println(my_pointer.country)

    // accessing struct field using dereferencing concept
    fmt.Println((*my_pointer).country)

}
```

The following will be the output for the above code:

```
&{New Delhi India}
India
India
```

The above program shows that you can pass the address of the `struct` to the pointer which represents the pointer to the `struct` concept. There is no need to use dereferencing explicitly as it will give the same result.

7.5.1 Updating value of struct member using pointer

You can also modify the values of the structure members or structure literals by using the pointer. Let's look at the following example:

```
Program 7.7
```

```go
// Golang program to update values of struct members using pointer

package main
```

```go
import "fmt"

type my_struct struct {
    city    string
    country string
}

func main() {

    // create instance of my_struct
    my_struct1 := my_struct{"New Delhi", "India"}

    // pointer to the struct
    my_pointer := &my_struct1

    // display struct values
    fmt.Println("Before updating value of struct member:\n", my_pointer)

    // update city name
    my_pointer.city = "Pune"
    fmt.Println("After updating value of struct member:\n", my_pointer)
}
```

The following will be the output for the above code:

```
Before updating value of struct member:
 &{New Delhi India}
After updating value of struct member:
 &{Pune India}
```

7.6 Exported vs. unexported structs and struct fields

Any `struct` type that starts with a capital letter is exported and accessible from outside packages. Similarly, any `struct` field that starts with a capital letter is exported and any `struct` type that starts with a small letter is visible only inside the same package.

Consider the following package hierarchy of a Go program:

```
program
    main
        main.go
    module
        city.go
        employee.go
```

You need to put the above folder structure and the Go programs in your GOPATH **directories.**

Let's look at the following program:

Program 7.8

city.go

```go
//non-main package
package module


// Unexported struct (accessible inside package module only)
type city struct {
    city_name string // unexported field(accessible inside package module
    only)
    state     string // unexported field(accessible inside package module
    only)
}


employee.go
//non-main package
package module
```

```go
type Employee struct { // exported struct type
    Id              int // exported field
    employee_name  string // unexported field(accessible inside package
    module)
    City           string // exported field
}
```

main.go
```go
//Go program with the main package
package main

import (
    "fmt"
    "program/module"
)

func main() {
    e := module.Employee{
        Id: 100,
        //employee_name: "Singh",
        City: "Pune",
    }
    fmt.Println("Employee ID and City= ", e)

    // c := module.city{
    // city_name: "Pune",
    // state:     "Maharashtra",
    // }
    // fmt.Println("City and State= ", c)

}
```

The following will be the output for the above code:

Employee ID and City= {100 Pune}

When you run `main.go`, the `Id` and `City` fields of the struct `Employee` are accessible from the outside package but the `employee_name` field is not accessible from it. An attempt to access `employee_name` struct fields from main would go through an error message because it starts with small letters.

When you run `main.go`, the `city_name` and `state` fields of the struct `city` are not accessible from the outside package. An attempt to access the `city_name` and `state` struct fields from main would go through an error message because they start with small letters.

7.7 Structs are value types

Structs are value types, i.e., when a value-type instance is created, a single space in memory is allocated to store the value.

When you assign one `struct` variable to another, a new copy of the `struct` is created and assigned. Similarly, when you pass a `struct` to another function, the function gets its copy of the `struct`. Let's look at the following program:

Program 7.9

```
//Go program to explain Structs are value types
package main

import "fmt"

type city struct {
    city1 string
    city2 string
    city3 string
}

func main() {
    // Structs are value types
    c1 := city{"Pune", "Delhi", "Lucknow"}
    c2 := c1 // A copy of the struct 'c1' is assigned to 'c2'
```

```
    fmt.Println("city list c1 =", c1)
    fmt.Println("city list c2 =", c2)


    c2.city2 = "Bengaluru"
    c2.city3 = "Mumbai"
    fmt.Println("\nAfter modifying c2:")
    fmt.Println("city list c1 =", c1)
    fmt.Println("city list c2 =", c2)
}
```

The following will be the output for the above code:

```
city list c1 = {Pune Delhi Lucknow}
city list c2 = {Pune Delhi Lucknow}

After modifying c2:
city list c1 = {Pune Delhi Lucknow}
city list c2 = {Pune Bengaluru Mumbai}
```

7.8 Struct equality

Two struct variables are equal if their corresponding fields are all equal. Let's look at the following example:

```
Program 7.10
//Go program to explain Structs equality
package main

import "fmt"

type city struct {
    city1 string
    city2 string
    city3 string
}
```

```go
func main() {
    // Two structs are equal if their corresponding fields are all equal.
    c1 := city{"Pune", "Delhi", "Lucknow"}
    c2 := city{"Pune", "Delhi", "Lucknow"}

    if c1 == c2 {
        fmt.Println("City list c1 and c2 are same")
    } else {
        fmt.Println("City list c1 and c2 are not same")
    }
}
```

The following will be the output for the above code:

`City list c1 and c2 are the same`

Conclusion

- In Go, a struct is a user-defined type that contains a collection of named fields and properties. It is used to group related data to form a single unit.

- Structs are the only way to create concrete user-defined types in the Go language and they also improve modularity.

- In Go, declaration of a struct starts with the keyword type, then a name for the new struct, and finally, the keyword `struct`. Within the curly brackets, a series of data fields are specified with a name and their types.

- You can initialize a variable of a struct type using a struct literal. You need to pass the field values in the same order in which they are declared in the struct.

- When a struct is defined and is not explicitly initialized with any value, the fields of the struct are assigned their zero values by default in the Go language.

- To access individual fields of a `struct`, you must use the dot (.) operator.

- A pointer in Go programming is a variable which is used to store the memory address of another variable. The variables are used to store some data at a memory address in the system.

- You can also use a pointer to a struct with the help of the & operator, i.e., the address operator. It is allowed to access the fields of a structure using the pointers without any dereferencing explicitly in Golang.

- In Go, any struct type that starts with a capital letter is exported and accessible from outside packages. Similarly, any struct field that starts with a capital letter is exported. Any struct type that starts with a small letter is visible only inside the same package.

- Structs are value types in Golang, i.e., when a value-type instance is created, a single space in memory is allocated to store the value. When you assign one struct variable to another, a new copy of the struct is created and assigned. Similarly, when you pass a struct to another function, the function gets its copy of the struct.

- Two struct variables are equal if their corresponding fields are all equal.

Questions

1. Write a Go program to declare and initialize a struct.

2. What is the zero value of a atruct? Write a Go program to explain the zero value of a struct.

3. Write a Go program to access the fields of a given struct.

4. How can we use a pointer to a struct? Write a Go program to explain the concept of pointer in struct.

5. Write a Go program to update the values of struct members using the pointer.

6. Explain how structs are value types using a Go program.

7. Write a Go program to check if two structs are equal.

CHAPTER 8
Methods

Methods are similar to functions. Methods are always associated with a type. Methods can be created for any data type. The data type can be basic type like int, bool, float32, etc. Or, it can be composite type like struct, slice, array map, etc. A method can access and modify the property of a type.

Structure

- Definition
- Value receiver and pointer receiver
- Methods of different types
- Methods of embedded type

Objective

This chapter covers the concept of methods in the Go programming language. You will learn how to declare a method, how to call a method, the syntax of different types of methods, and the method resolution process.

8.1 Definition

The syntax of methods is almost similar to function with one difference— the method always has a receiver between the `func` keyword and the method name as shown below:

```
func (receiverName receiverType) methodName(param1 paramType) (returnType1) {
    ...
}
```

The receiver is placed in parenthesis `()` after the `func` keyword and before the method name. The rest of the syntax is similar to the function. It has a list of parameters. A method can have a single or multiple parameters. There can be multiple method parameters with different types, or all parameters can be of the same type. The same is applied to the return types. However, if a method returns multiple values, then the return type must be in parenthesis; otherwise, we can omit the parenthesis.

You might be wondering why we need a receiver on a method. We don't need a receiver in other class-based object-oriented languages like C++ and Java. This is because methods are grouped into classes in C++ and Java. Methods are always declared as part of the class body. So the compiler can understand by class definition that the class has certain methods in it. But this is not the case with Go. Type and its methods are not grouped. Methods are not part of its type declaration. Even methods don't need to be in the same source file as their type. You can declare methods and their type both in different source files. So, we need a receiver on a method so that the Go compiler can understand which type it is a part of.

The most crucial point to note here is that methods and their type must be declared in the same package. You cannot declare a method in a different package than its type. This is the reason we that we cannot add a method to predefined named types. Example: You cannot add a method to `time.Duration`. However, there is a workaround for this which we will see in a later section.

Program 8.1

```
type rectangle struct {
    length float32
    width  float32
}
func (r rectangle) area() float32 {
    return r.length * r.width
}
```

Program 8.1 declares a struct named rectangle with field length and width. Both length and width are declared as float32. The rectangle struct has a method named as area(). The method is not declared as part of the rectangle body. Instead, it is declared separately. It is considered a method of the rectangle struct because the rectangle is used as the receiver type. The receiver is placed between the func keyword and the method name area(). The receiver is declared with the receiver variable r. We can access fields of the receiver in a method body by applying the dot (.) operator on the receiver variable. We have accessed length and width in the method body by r.length and r.width. The method calculates the area of the rectangle by multiplying length and area and finally, it returns the result. The return type of the method is float32.

You can give any valid identifier as a receiver name. You can define a receiver name as *this* or *self* like we define in Java or Python respectively, but it is not mandatory. It is also possible to define different receiver names for all methods. It is a good practice to give short and the same names for all receivers. *Program 8.2* declares two methods, area and perimeter, and both the methods have different receiver names, r and rect respectively.

Program 8.2

```
type rectangle struct {
    length float32
    width  float32
}
func (r rectangle) area() float32 {
    return r.length * r.width
}
func (rect rectangle) perimeter() float32 {
    return (2 * rect.length) + (2 * rect.width)
}
```

The receiver name is not mandatory in the method declaration. You can declare a method by providing receiver type only. If a method does not read or modify any field of the receiver, we can omit the receiver name (though it is not a valid usecase because if a method does read/modify the field, then there is no point in declaring that method).

Program 8.3 declares a method name doSomething with the receiver type only. This method does not read/modify any field of rectangle struct. Instead, it just prints a string on the console, so we have removed the receiver variable as shown below:

Program 8.3

```
type rectangle struct {
    length float32
    width  float32
}
func (rectangle) doSomething() {
    fmt.Println("I don't know what to do")
}
```

Till now, we have learned how to declare a method. Now, let's learn how to call a method. The method can be called using the dot (.) operator on type value. The code given below calls the area() method on rect variable of rectangle struct. It returns a float32 value, so we have assigned it to variable a. Finally, it prints the result on the console:

Program 8.4

```
func main() {
    rect := rectangle{12.3, 21.45}
    a := rect.area()
    fmt.Println(a)
}
```

Putting all together

Program 8.5

```
package main
import "fmt"
func main() {
    rect := rectangle{12.3, 21.45}
    a := rect.area()
    fmt.Println(a)
}
type rectangle struct {
    length float32
```

```
      width   float32
}
func (r rectangle) area() float32 {
      return r.length * r.width
}
func (r rectangle) perimeter() float32 {
      return (2 * r.length) + (2 * r.width)
}
```

8.2 Value receiver and pointer receiver

We have used value receivers in all examples in *Section 8.1*. We are trying to read values from the value receiver. However, if we try to modify values on the value receiver, it will not reflect in the caller because the modification is done by value receiver in method and changes are not visible to the caller. Let us verify this in the following program:

```
Program 8.6
package main
import "fmt"
func main() {
      rect := rectangle{12.3, 21.45}
      rect.increaseLength(3.4)
      fmt.Println(rect)
}
type rectangle struct {
      length float32
      width   float32
}
func (r rectangle) increaseLength(a float32) {
      r.length = r.length + a
}
```

The following will be the output for the above program:

```
{12.3 21.45}
```

Program 8.6 adds a new method, increaseLength, with value receiver. This method increases the length of the rectangle by the input provided. The main method creates a variable, rect, for the rectangle struct with the length and width values as 12.3 and 21.45, respectively. The main method calls the increaseLength method by passing 3.4 as a parameter. Finally, it prints the rect on the console. According to the code, it should print rect with the updated length but that is not true. It prints {12.3 21.45} on the console where the length is still 12.3. The reason for this is very simple. The increaseLength is defined with the value receiver.

What if you want to modify the receiver and want the changes to be visible to the caller? You can use a pointer receiver. The syntax for a method with pointer receiver is similar to the method with values except for one difference, i.e., receiver defined as a pointer. Please note the syntax given below. The receiverType is prefixed with an asterisk (*).

```
func (receiverName *receiverType) methodName(param1 paramType) (returnType1) {
    ...
}
```

Let us redeclare the increaseLength method with a pointer receiver:

Program 8.7

```
package main
import "fmt"
func main() {
    rect := rectangle{12.3, 21.45}
    p := &rect
    p.increaseLength(3.4)
    fmt.Println(rect)
}
type rectangle struct {
    length float32
    width  float32
}
func (r *rectangle) increaseLength(a float32) {
    r.length = r.length + a
}
```

The following will be the output for the above program:

```
{15.7 21.45}
```

When you run this program, it will print the updated value, 15.7, for length. The most important point to note here is that the increaseLength method is called with a pointer to rect.

It is not mandatory to call pointer receiver methods with the pointer variable. You can call these methods with a non-pointer variable. The Go compiler will get the address of a variable when a pointer receiver method is called without a pointer. The reverse is also true. You can call a value receiver method with a pointer variable. Go dereferences automatically when it finds the pointer is being used to value the receiver method. Referencing and dereferencing only works when variables are used. The Go compiler cannot perform referencing and dereferencing when there is no variable found. The following program gives compilation errors:

Program 8.8

```
func main() {
    rectangle{12.3, 21.45}.increaseLength(3.5)
}
```

The following will be the output for the above program:

Error 8.1:

cannot call the pointer method on composite literal

cannot take the address of composite literal

A type can have a mix of a pointer receiver and value receiver method. But it is the best practice to have either all pointer receiver methods or all value receiver methods. Think before you choose a value receiver. The pointer receiver is always better than a value receiver for two reasons:

1. When a method is called with a value receiver, a copy of the instance gets created and then passed to the method. It is very costly when an instance is very big. It is always a good practice to pass the pointer receiver because it passes the address instead of a full copy.
2. If you are very confident that this method is being called from limited places and that this method will not be required to update the receiver in the future, only then you should choose the value receiver. Otherwise, you should select the pointer receiver.

A type can have a mix of a value receiver and pointer receiver methods. Some methods can be declared as value receiver and some methods can be declared as pointer receiver on a type. It's always a good practice to have either all methods as value receiver or pointer receiver. We should not mix both of them unless it is extremely necessary.

8.3 Methods of different types

Till now, we have added methods to a `struct` type. However, methods are not limited to the `struct`. You can define methods to any type like basic types: `int`, `float32`, `string`, `bool`, etc., and other composite types: `array`, `slice`, `map`, etc. It is also possible to define a method on function.

8.3.1 Method on the basic type

It is not possible to define a method on the basic type directly. We need to create a custom type first. In *Program 8.9*, we have created a custom type, `number`, of `int` type. Then we have created three methods on the number. `isPrime` and `isDivisible` are declared as value receivers because these methods do not modify the receiver, whereas `increaseBy` is declared as the pointer receiver. After all, it modifies the receiver. The method `increaseBy` takes a number type parameter and adds it to the receiver. When the caller prints the receiver after the method call, it prints the updated value. The method `isPrime` doesn't take any parameters but returns `bool` value and it returns true if the receiver is prime, otherwise it returns false. The method `isDivisible` takes a number type parameter and it returns the `bool` type. It returns true if the receiver is divisible by the provided parameter and false otherwise.

Program 8.9

```
package main

import "fmt"

func main() {
    var n number = 7
    fmt.Println(n.isPrime())
    fmt.Println(n.isDivisible(3))
    n.increamentBy(3)
    fmt.Println(n)
}


type number int


func (n number) isPrime() bool {
    for i := 2; i < int(n); i++ {
        if int(n)%i == 0 {
```

```
        return false
      }
    }
    return true
}
func (n number) isDivisible(i number) bool {
    return (n % i) == 0
}
func (n *number) increamentBy(i number) {
    *n = *n + i
}
```

The following will be the output for the above program:

true

false

10

8.3.2 Method on composite types

We will define methods on the slice in this section. Like int, we need to define a custom type of slice to define methods on it.

```
Program 8.10
package main
import "fmt"
func main() {
    var l list = []string{"A", "B", "C"}
    var input list = []string{"B", "C", "D"}
    intersResult := l.intersect(input)
    fmt.Println("Intersection:", intersResult)
    l.remove("B")
    fmt.Println("After deletion:", l)
    fmt.Println("Index of B:", l.indexOf("B"))
    fmt.Println("Index of C:", l.indexOf("C"))
}
```

```go
type list []string
func (l list) intersect(input list) list {
    mp := make(map[string]bool)
    for _, ele := range l {
        mp[ele] = true
    }
    var result list
    for _, ele := range input {
        if mp[ele] {
            result = append(result, ele)
        }
    }
    return result
}
func (l *list) remove(in string) {
    index := l.indexOf(in)
    *l = append((*l)[:index], (*l)[index+1:]...)
}


func (l list) indexOf(in string) int {
    for index, ele := range l {
        if ele == in {
            return index
        }
    }
    return -1
}
```

The following will be the output for the above program:

Intersection: [B C]

After deletion: [A C]

Index of B: -1

```
Index of C: 1
```

Program 8.10 has defined a custom type, `list`, of the slice. The `list` type has three methods: `intersect`, `remove`, and `indexOf`. The `intersect` method takes a list as a parameter and returns the list which is an intersection of the receiver list and parameter list. It doesn't modify the receiver. The `indexOf` method takes a string as a parameter and returns the `int` value. It finds the index of the provided parameter in the list. The `remove` method takes a string as a parameter and doesn't return anything. This is a pointer receiver method because it removes the provided parameter from the receiver.

The main function defines two variables of list type, i.e., `l` and `input`. It calls the intersect method on l by passing `input` as a parameter. Then, it prints the returned result. It also calls the `remove` method bypassing `B` as a parameter, and then it prints the l, which doesn't print the `B`.

8.3.3 Method on the function type

We can define methods on function type also. This feature is used a lot in `stdlib`. One good example of `stdlib` is `net/http` package. This package has a function type as shown below:

```
type HandlerFunc func(ResponseWriter, *Request)
```

The `HandleFunc` method type has a method `ServeHTTP` as below:

```
func (f HandlerFunc) ServeHTTP(w ResponseWriter, r *Request)
```

The method on the function is very useful when we need to provide similar functionality with multiple scenarios. The following code does the same thing. This code has a `Filter` method on the `By` function type. The `Filter` method filters the user's slice by age, most liked, most visited, and most followed.

Program 8.11

```
package main


import "fmt"


type User struct {
    id          int
    name        string
```

```go
    age         int
    visitDays   int
    totalLikes  int
    followers   int
}

var users []User = []User{
    User{101, "A", 18, 20, 645, 2342},
    User{102, "B", 23, 110, 323, 110},
    User{103, "C", 40, 125, 1120, 4577},
    User{104, "D", 36, 45, 323, 1201},
    User{105, "D", 42, 45, 323, 1201},
}

type By func(user User) bool

func (by By) Filter(s1 []User) []User {
    filtered := make([]User, 0)
    for _, ele := range s1 {
        if by(ele) {
            filtered = append(filtered, ele)
        }
    }
    return filtered
}

func main() {

    //Frequent User
    frequent := func(user User) bool {
        return user.visitDays > 100
    }
```

```
//Liked User

appreciated := func(user User) bool {

    return user.totalLikes > 500

}


// Large followers

respected := func(user User) bool {

    return user.followers > 1000

}


// Matured User

matured := func(user User) bool {

    return user.age > 35

}
frequestUsers := By(frequent).Filter(users)

fmt.Println(frequestUsers)


appreciatedUsers := By(appreciated).Filter(users)

fmt.Println(appreciatedUsers)


respectedUsers := By(respected).Filter(users)

fmt.Println(respectedUsers)


maturedUsers := By(matured).Filter(users)

fmt.Println(maturedUsers)

}
```

We have created a struct named User with fields id, name, age, visitedDays, totalLiks, and followers. We have a users variable which is a slice of User and has stored five user values into it. By is a function type that accepts the User type as a parameter and returns bool type. The Filter is a method on the By function type which has a slice of User as a parameter and returns a slice of User. The Filter method returns a filtered user based on it is called on the actual value of the By type function. It iterates over s1 (the User slice) and calls the by function in the if condition. The by value within the if condition returns true or false based on its implementation. The main function defines four values for the By function type, i.e., frequent, appreciated, respected, and matured. All these values have their implementation for the By function type. The frequent function returns true if the total number of the visit is more than 100. The appreciated function returns true if the total number of likes are more than 500. The respected function returns true if the total number of followers is more than 1000. The matured function returns true of the age is more than 35.

All the function values are converted into the By type before calling the Filter method on these. So, the conclusion is that the functionality of Filter is reused. One filter functionality can be applied to a different type of filter, therefore it is reused. We don't have to rewrite or duplicate filter functions for different types of conditions.

8.4 Methods of embedded type

Inheritance is the most important pillar of OOPs, but Go does not have an inheritance (IS-A), i.e., there is no parent-child relationship. We can achieve a similar feature by using embedding (HAS-A). We need to embed a type within type without specifying the variable name as shown below:

Program 8.12

```
package main


import "fmt"


type Person struct {
    id        int
    firstName  string
    lastName   string
}


func (p Person) getFullName() string {
    return p.firstName + " " + p.lastName
}
```

```
type Student struct {

    Person

    marks []float32

}


func (s Student) getTotalMarks() (total float32) {

    for _, val := range s.marks {

        total += val

    }

    return

}


func main() {

    p := Person{101, "Prithvi", "Singh"}

    marks := []float32{10.2, 23.3, 19.5}

    s := Student{p, marks}

    fmt.Println(s.getFullName())

    fmt.Println(s.getTotalMarks())

}
```

We have declared the Person struct with fields id, firstName, and lastName. The Person struct has one method, getFirstName which returns the full name by combining the firstName and lastName. We have declared one more struct, i.e., Student with field marks and method getTotalMarks(). The Person is embedded in the Student. Please note here that we have not defined the variable name for the Person in Student. In the main function, we have declared the value s for Student type. Please also note here that we are calling the getFullName() method on the Student's variable. Like inheritance, it is directly available in Student type. This is called method **promotion**.

We can also call the getFullName() method on the Student type by specifying the Person:

s.Person.getFullName()

8.4.1 Method resolution process

The compiler uses the method resolution process to find the method. When a method is called on a type, it first tries to find it in the same type. If it is not found in the same type, it looks into all the embedded types; if none of the embedded types have that method, it tries to find in the embedded of embedded type:

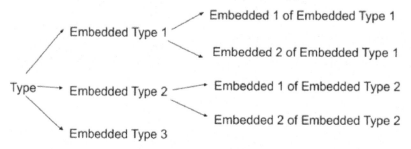

Figure 8.1: Method resolution process

If a method is defined in two embedded types at the same level, then that is ambiguity. So the compiler gives a compilation error:

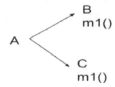

Figure 8.2: Ambiguity in the method resolution process

In *Program 8.13*, the method m1() is defined in B and C types. Both B and C are embedded in A. It gives a compilation error in main() function when m1() is called on a variable of A. This is because when the compiler does not find the m1() method in A, it tried to find in the embedded type, i.e., B and C. But m1() is defined in both B and C.

Program 8.13

```
package main

type A struct {
    B
    C
}
type B struct {
```

```
}
func (b B) m1() {

}


type C struct {

}
func (c C) m1() {

}
func main() {
    a := A{}
    a.m1()

}
```

The following will be the output for the above program:

Error 8.2: ./main.go:20:3: ambiguous selector a.m1

This can be resolved by specifying the embedded type while calling the method. If we want to call the m1 method of C, then we can specify C on variable a by dot operator and then the method name. Given below is the example:

`a.C.m1()`

There will not be any problem when the same method is defined on the embedded type but at different levels. If B and C are embedded in A and D is embedded in B, the m1() method is defined in C and D which are at different levels. There is no ambiguity in this case. When m1() is called on the variable of A, it will always call m1() of C:

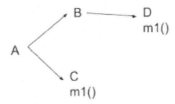

Figure 8.3: *No ambiguity in the method resolution process*

```
Program 8.14
package main
import "fmt"
type A struct {
    B
```

```
        C
}
type B struct {
        D
}


type D struct {
}


func (d D) m1() {
        fmt.Println("m1 of D")
}


type C struct {
}


func (c C) m1() {
        fmt.Println("m1 of C")
}
func main() {
        a := A{}
        a.m1()
}
```

If we want to call the m1() method of D, then we can specify it explicitly:

```
a.B.D.m1()
```

If there is no ambiguity in B's hierarchy, we can chain it till B and the method resolution will start from a.B. The statements given above and below have the same behavior. Both will execute m1() method on D:

```
a.B.m1()
```

8.4.2 Polymorphism is not allowed

Polymorphism is not allowed on embedded types. It can be achieved by an interface; we will cover interface in the next chapter. Let's take an example of Person and Student. The Person is embedded in Student. If a function expects a Person as a parameter, we cannot pass the value of the Student:

Program 8.15

```go
package main

type Person struct {
    id   int
    name string
}
type Student struct {
    Person
    marks []float32
}
func processPerson(person Person) {
}
func main() {
    s := Student{Person{101, "Prithvi"}, []float32{9.3, 3.4, 6.7}}
    processPerson(s)
}
```

The following will be the output for the above program:

Error 8.3:

./main.go:16:15: cannot use s (type Student) as type Person in argument to processPerson

In *Program 8.15*, we have defined Person with id and name fields and Student with Person as embedded and marks. There is a function processPerson() which expects a Person as a parameter. We have created a value of Student type and have tried to pass it to the processPerson() function. It gives a compilation error saying that we cannot use Student type as Person type in the argument to processPerson.

We can call the processPerson() function by passing Person value which is part of Student value:

```
processPerson(s.Person)
```

Method overloading is also not allowed in Go. The compiler will complain if we try to do method overloading.

Conclusion

- Declaration of function and method are almost similar. There is only one difference in their declaration—method declaration contains receiver whereas the function does not.
- Methods can always be associated with any type. We can specify that type by the receiver.
- We cannot declare a method without a type of body. We can declare a method to type anywhere.
- We declare a method to a type when we want to modify and get properties of the type.
- There are two types of receivers:
  o **Pointer receiver**: It is used when we want to modify the properties of the type.
  o **Value receiver**: It is used when we want to get the properties of the type. The modification done by the value receiver method does not reflect outside of the methods.
- We can declare methods on the basic data type, composite type, and even on function.
- A method can be called using the dot (.) operator on an instance of the type.
- If a method is available in embedded type, then Golang uses the method resolution process to find a method. There can be ambiguity if a method is found in two types embedded at the same level.

Questions

1. What is the output of the following code?

```go
package main

import "fmt"

type person struct {
    id    int
    name string
}

func (p person) setName(name string) {
    p.name = name
}

func main() {
    p := person{101, "Xyz"}
    p.setName("Abc")
    fmt.Println(p)
}
```

2. State true or false:

    a. We can create an overloaded method in Golang.

    b. The pointer receiver method can only be called on the address of the type on which the method is declared.

    c. We can create a method without specifying a receiver variable. The receiver type is enough to declare a method.

    d. It is not necessary to declare a method of a type in the same file where the type is declared.

3. Write a program to define the following custom types of int: Distance, Millimeter, Centimeter, Meter, Kilometer. You need to add methods on each type to convert and return the values of other types. For example, you can define methods on Millimeter to convert its value to Centimeter, Meter, and Kilometer.

4. Consider the program from question 1. What will be the output if we call the setName() method on the address of the person type?

5. Find the problem in the following program:

```go
package main
import "fmt"
type A struct {
}
func (a A) m1() {
   fmt.Println("M1 of A")
}
type B struct {
   A
}
func (b B) m1(a int) {
   fmt.Println("M1 of B")
}
func main() {
   b := B{}
   b.m1()
}
```

CHAPTER 9
Interfaces

Interfaces provide pure abstraction in Golang. The interface body can have only method declaration and embedded interfaces. The methods in the interface do not have the body and only the method signature can be defined in the interface. We cannot create an object of an interface. The interfaces are meant for the implementation. Any type which implements provides the body of the method.

Structure

- Introduction
- Implementing an interface
- Empty interface
- Method set
- Frequently used built-in/stdlib interfaces
- Interface with struct
- Some important points

Objective

This chapter will cover the concept of interface in Golang. You will learn what the interface is in Golang, how Golang interfaces are different from other languages, how to declare an interface, how implicit implementation happens in Golang, and its benefits. We will create the interface without methods and see its benefits with built-in functions. We will see the impact of the value receiver and pointer receiver while implementing the interface and creating polymorphic objects.

9.1 Introduction

The syntax of interface is similar to struct. The following is the syntax:

```
type InterfaceName interface{
    MethodName(argument argumentType) returnType
}
```

The above syntax has a method that has one argument and one return type. Argument type and return type should be valid Go types. The type defined in the above syntax is just to explain the syntax.

Program 9.1 has a valid syntax:

```
Program 9.1
type Executor interface {
    Execute()
}
```

The interface name is Executor. It has one method, i.e., Execute(). The method does not have an argument and does not return anything. If an interface has only one method, then it is an interface naming convention that interface name should be methodName plus [e]r. In our example, the method name is Execute. So, the interface name is Executor, by appending r at the end of the method name. It is not a hardcore rule but it is a convention.

There can be multiple methods in an interface. All methods can have a different signature. The code given below has defined an interface called Connection. You can understand from the definition of the interface that it can be implemented by any type which can connect to some external resources like database, socket, etc. It has two methods, i.e., Open and Close. The Open() method expects string URI which is used to connect. It returns two values: session and error. The Close() method does not expect any argument but it returns the error type.

Program 9.2

```go
type Connection interface {

    Open(uri string) (Session, error)

    Close() error

}
```

9.2 Implementing an interface

As we just discussed, an interface is purely abstract. Its method does not have the body. We cannot create a value/object of an interface. The whole purpose of an interface is that some types will implement it. There is no keyword to implement an interface. Implementing an interface is implicit in Go. If a type has all the methods which are defined in an interface, then it implements that interface by default.

Program 9.3

```go
package main


import "fmt"


type Executor interface {

    Execute()

}


type Thread struct {

}


func (t Thread) Execute() {

    fmt.Println("Executing thread")

}

func main() {

    var exe Executor

    exe = Thread{}

    exe.Execute()

}
```

The following will be the output of the above program:

Executing thread

The `Thread` type in the above code implements the `Executor` interface implicitly. Unlike Java, we have not used any specific keyword to implement the interface. What is the proof that Thread implements the `Executor`? The answer is in the main function. We have created a polymorphic object of Thread. We have defined a variable of `Executor`, i.e., exe and assigned an object of Thread to it.

If the `Execute()` method was not defined in the `Thread` type, we would have gotten a compilation error in the main method while creating a polymorphic object.

cannot use (Thread literal) (value of type Thread) as Executor value in the assignment: missing method Execute

As we have seen in *Program 9.3*, we can create a variable of an interface and assign actual implementation value to it. If we don't assign actual implementation value to the `interface` variable, the interface variable will be useless because the variable will be assigned nil. If we call the method on that variable, the code will panic. If we modify the above code and remove the assignment of Thread to exe, then this code will panic and generate the following error message:

Error 9.1:

```
panic: runtime error: invalid memory address or nil pointer dereference
[signal SIGSEGV: segmentation violation code=0x1 addr=0x0 pc=0x108909f]
goroutine 1 [running]:
main.main()
    /Users/prithvipalsingh/go/src/workspace/main.go:17 +0x1f
exit status 2
```

To implement any interface, you need to define/override all the methods of the interface in the type. We will get a compilation error in the main function of the code given below because we have defined only the `Close()` method of `Connection` in `DbConnection`. The `Open()` method is missing.

Program 9.4

```go
package main

import "fmt"

type Session struct {
```

```
}

type Connection interface {
    Open(uri string) (Session, error)
    Close() error
}

type DbConnection struct {
}

func (conn DbConnection) Close() error {
    fmt.Println("Closing Database Connection")
    return nil
}

func main() {
    var conn Connection
    conn = DbConnection{}
    conn.Close()
}
```

The following will be the error in the above program:

**Error 9.2:cannot use (DbConnection literal) (value of type DbConnection)
as Connection value in assignment: missing method Open**

You can resolve this error by defining the Open() method in the DbConnection type.

9.2.1 Why implicit implementation?

If you come from a Java background, you might be wondering why we are doing implicit implementation of the interface. You might be thinking that explicit implementation is always proper as that becomes clear by looking at the type that implements which interface. But implicit implementation has its benefits:

- You may want to implement your custom interface in type which is available in a third-party library. You don't have access to the code, so you can't change the code. The implicit implementation is beneficial in this case. If the type has methods that can satisfy your interface, it implements that interface implicitly.

- If you want to create a new interface with very few methods and you want to implement that interface in many types, you don't need to make code changes in all the places.

9.2.2 Polymorphism: Interface as a contract

We have already seen that if a type satisfies the interface, we can assign the value of that to the variable of the interface. So, if a function has an interface as a parameter, we can pass a value of any type which satisfies that interface. The interface behaves as a contract between the function and caller of the function. The function doesn't know anything about actual implementation that is being passed to the function. It only knows that it can call all the methods of the interface. The call will go to the implementation. The caller of the function can only pass the type which has all the methods of the interface.

There is a phrase that fits perfectly the interface as a contract: If something can do this, then it can be used here.

Program 9.5

```go
package main

import "fmt"

type Bird interface {
    Fly()
}

type Eagle struct {
}

func (e Eagle) Fly() {
    fmt.Println("Eagle is flying over the cloud")
}

type Pigeon struct {
```

```go
}

func (p Pigeon) Fly() {
    fmt.Println("Pigeon is flying on normal height")
}

type Penguin struct {
}

func (p Penguin) Fly() {
    fmt.Println("Penguin cannot fly")
}

func flyNow(b Bird) {
    b.Fly()
}

func main() {
    flyNow(Eagle{})
    flyNow(Pigeon{})
    flyNow(Penguin{})
}
```

The following will be the output for the above program:

Eagle is flying over the cloud

Pigeon is flying on normal height

Penguin cannot fly

We have created an interface named Bird. The Bird interface has a method Fly().
We have created three structs (Eagle, Pigeon, Penguin) and all implement Bird by
overriding Fly() methods. Most importantly, we have defined a function as flyNow().
The flyNow function expects Bird as an argument and calls the Fly method on the
variable of Bird. The flyNow function does not know which implementation of Bird
will be passed; it only knows that the implementation will have a Fly method. We
can pass an object of any type which implements the Bird interface. In the main()

function, we are calling the flyNow function three times and we have passed the value of Eagle, Pigeon, Penguin. When the flyNow function calls the Fly method, its actual call goes to the Eagle, Pigeon, or Penguin.

9.3 Empty interface

Till now, we have seen that if a type has all the methods of an interface, it means that it satisfies the interface and it implements the interface implicitly. But what if an interface doesn't have any method? In this case, all types satisfy the interface. The interface without any method is called the empty interface.

Since all the types satisfy the empty interface, we can assign the value of any type to the variable of the interface.

Program 9.6

```go
package main

import "fmt"
type MyEmpty interface {
}

type Student struct {
    id   int
    name string
}

func main() {
    var empty MyEmpty
    empty = 10
    fmt.Println(empty)
    empty = "a"
    fmt.Println(empty)
    empty = 22.3
    fmt.Println(empty)
    empty = Student{101, "Shyam"}
    fmt.Println(empty)
```

```
}
```

The following will be the output for the above program:

```
10
```

```
a
```

```
22.3
```

```
{101 Shyam}
```

We have created an empty interface called `MyEmpty`. The interface `MyEmpty` doesn't have any method. We have also created a `Student` struct with `id` and `name` as fields. In the main function, we have created a variable of `MyEmpty` interface with the name empty. We have assigned different types of values to this variable like `int`, `string`, `float32`, and `Student`. We have also printed these values.

But what is the benefit of an empty interface? We will understand the benefit of it by looking at the standard library code. We frequently use the `fmt` package to print output on the console. Have you ever tried to understand how the `fmt.Println()` function works? Why does it allow us to pass any of the values? Let us first look at the signature of this function:

```
func Println(a ...interface{}) (n int, err error) {
    return Fprintln(os.Stdout, a...)
}
```

Please notice the parameter of the function. It accepts `var-args` of an empty interface. So, `var-args` means that you can pass any number of arguments and an empty interface means you can pass the value of any type.

9.4 Method set

The method set is a set of method that makes a type implicitly implement an interface. Till now, we have seen that when a type defines all the methods of an interface, that type implicitly implements all the methods of that interface. But we have not seen whether the method should be a pointer receiver or value receiver method. The interface methods do not specify whether the implementing type should have a pointer receiver or value receiver.

If a type `T` has pointer receiver methods (of an interface), then `*T` implements the interface and not `T`. We can assign the address of `T` to interface variable. If we try to assign the value of `T` to an interface variable, we will get a compilation error. Let us understand this by the following program:

Program 9.7

```go
package main

import "fmt"

type Itr interface {
    m1()
    m2()
}
type St struct {
}

func (s *St) m1() {
    fmt.Println("In m1 of St")
}
func (s *St) m2() {
    fmt.Println("In m2 of St")
}
func main() {
    var i Itr
    i = St{}
    i.m1()
    i.m2()
}
```

The following will be the error in the above program:

Error 9.3:

./main.go:20:4: cannot use St literal (type St) as type Itr in assignment:

St does not implement Itr (m1 method has pointer receiver)

In *Program 9.7*, we have defined an interface as Itr. This interface has two methods: m1 and m2. We have defined a struct type as St. The type St implements the Itr interface by defining m1 and m2 methods with a pointer receiver. In the main function, we have declared a variable of Itr using the var keyword and we have assigned the value of St to it. Then, we have called the m1 and m2 methods on the interface variable. But when we run this code, we get a compilation error. The error says that St does not implement Itr. The reason behind this error is that *St implements Itr interface, not St.

If we re-run the above code by assigning the address of St to the variable i, the code will work just fine.

When we implement an interface by a value receiver, we can assign both the value and address of the type to the interface. Let us see this in the following code:

```
Program 9.8
package main
import "fmt"
type Itr interface {
    m1()
    m2()
}
type St struct {
}

func (s St) m1() {
    fmt.Println("In m1 of St")
}
func (s St) m2() {
    fmt.Println("In m2 of St")
}
func main() {
    var i Itr
    fmt.Println("Assigning value of St")
    i = St{}
    i.m1()
    i.m2()
    fmt.Println("Assigning Address of St")
    i = &St{}
    i.m1()
```

```
    i.m2()
}
```

The following will be the output for the above program:

```
Assigning value of St

In m1 of St

In m2 of St

Assigning Address of St

In m1 of St

In m2 of St
```

In the above code, we have implemented the Itr interface by defining the m1 and m2 methods with values receiver. In the main function, we have tried to assign both the value and address of St to an interface variable and it worked fine. We will not get a compilation error in this code.

Conclusion of method set:

1. If a type T implements an interface I by defining the pointer receiver methods, then only *T will implement interface I, not T. So, we can assign only the address of T to the interface variable.

2. If a type T implements an interface I by defining a value receiver, then both T and *T implement the interface I. So, we can assign both the value and address of T to the interface variable.

9.5 Frequently used built-in/stdlib interfaces

There are too many frequently used interfaces in the standard library. We cannot cover all those interfaces here. We will cover the Stringer interface in this section and we will see the error interface implementation in *Section 12.1.2*.

9.5.1 Stringer interface

The Stringer interface is very useful for printing customized output. It has only one method called String which returns a string. When we print a value of a type using fmt.Println(), if the type overrides the String() method, the String() method gets called internally. The fmt package will print whatever the String() method returns.

Program 9.9

```go
package main
import "fmt"


type Dollar float64
func (d Dollar) String() string {
    return fmt.Sprintf("$%f", d)
}
func main() {
    var d Dollar = 23.3
    fmt.Println(d)
}
```

The following will be the output for the above program:

$23.300000

We have created a new type of float64, i.e., Dollar. The Dollar type overrides the String() method of the Stringer interface. The String() method returns the value of Dollar with prefixing the $. The main function creates a new variable, d, of type Dollar, and assigns 23.3 to it. When we print d, it prints $23.300000 on the console.

9.5.2 Interface interface of sort package

There is an interface in the Golang standard library called Interface. Please note that the interface name itself is Interface. This interface is defined in the sort package and used for sorting slices of user-defined types. This interface has three methods: Len, Swap, and Less. The code snippet given below is the definition of the Interface interface from the sort package:

Program 9.10

```go
package sort


type Interface interface {
    Len() int
    Less(i, j int) bool
    Swap(i, j int)
}
```

If we want to sort a slice of any type, then we need to call the Sort function of sort package. The Sort function expects the Interface type. So, we can pass any type which implements Interface. The type can implement the Interface interface by implementing all three methods:

Program 9.11

```go
package main
import (
    "fmt"
    "sort"
)
type Student struct {
    Name   string
    Marks int
}
func (s Student) String() string {
    return fmt.Sprintf("%s: %d", s.Name, s.Marks)
}
type ByMarks []Student
func (b ByMarks) Len() int        { return len(b) }
func (b ByMarks) Swap(i, j int) { b[i], b[j] = b[j], b[i] }
func (b ByMarks) Less(i, j int) bool {
    return b[i].Marks < b[j].Marks
}
func main() {
    students := []Student{
        {"Bob", 31},
        {"John", 42},
        {"Michael", 17},
        {"Jenny", 26},
    }
    fmt.Println("Before sorting =", students)
    sort.Sort(ByMarks(students))
    fmt.Println("After sorting =", students)
```

```
}
```

The following will be the output for the above program:

Before sorting = [Bob: 31 John: 42 Michael: 17 Jenny: 26]

After sorting = [Michael: 17 Jenny: 26 Bob: 31 John: 42]

In *Program 9.11,* we have declared a struct called `Student`. We have defined the `String()` method in `Student` to print `Student` objects in a beautified way. Then, we have created a new type of Student slice, i.e., `ByMarks` and we have defined all three methods of interface on `ByMarks` type as follows:

- `Len`: It returns the length of the slice.

- `Swap`: It swaps ith index element with jth index element.

- `Less`: It has logic to find which element is less between the ith index element and jth.

In the main function, we have a slice of `Student` with four elements. When we print `students` variable, it prints in the sequence in which these elements were inserted. In the next line, we are sorting the students variable by passing the `sort.Sort()` function. We have typecasted to the `ByMarks` type before passing it to the `sort.Sort()` function.

The above is unnecessarily complicated for sorting. The `Len` and `Swap` methods are unnecessary because the `Sort` function should have an internal logic to find the length of the `slice` and swap elements. The `sort` package has a function to overcome this complexity. We can use the `Slice` function of the sort package. We will not need to implement any `Interface`. The sort. `Slice` function expects two parameters:

1. The slice of the elements that we want to sort.

2. The function that will have logic for sorting.

The following code demonstrates the `sort.Slice` function:

Program 9.12

```
package main


import (
    "fmt"
    "sort"
)
```

```go
type Student struct {
    Name   string
    Marks  int
}


func (s Student) String() string {
    return fmt.Sprintf("%s: %d", s.Name, s.Marks)
}


func main() {
    students := []Student{
        {"Bob", 31},
        {"John", 42},
        {"Michael", 17},
        {"Jenny", 26},
    }
    fmt.Println("Before sorting", students)
    sort.Slice(students, func(i, j int) bool {
        return students[i].Marks < students[j].Marks
    })
    fmt.Println("After sorting", students)
}
```

The following will be the output for the above program:

Before sorting [Bob: 31 John: 42 Michael: 17 Jenny: 26]

After sorting [Michael: 17 Jenny: 26 Bob: 31 John: 42]

In *Program 9.12*, the Student struct does not implement any interface. This code calls the sort.Slice() method. We have passed a slice of students and an anonymous function. The anonymous function has logic to sort students by Marks in ascending order.

9.6 Interface with struct

An `Interface` can be used within a struct body. We can either use the interface as an embedded type or we can define an interface variable. We cannot pass the actual value of an interface while creating a struct value because interfaces are abstract. We need to pass the value of the actual implementation type. So, when we call a method of the interface on a struct, the call will go to the actual implementation type.

9.6.1 Interface variable as struct field

An interface variable can be used as a `struct` field. When an object of that `struct` is created, we need to pass the actual implementation value for the interface as shown below:

Program 9.13

```go
package main

import "fmt"

type Executor interface {
    Execute()
}
type Thread struct {
}
func (t Thread) Execute() {
    fmt.Println("Executing thread")
}
type Process struct {
    exe Executor
}

func main() {
    p := Process{Thread{}}
    p.exe.Execute()
}
```

The following will be the output for the above program:

Executing thread

In *Program 9.13*, we have created a struct called Process with the interface variable, exe, as a field. The exe field is a variable of the Executor interface. The Thread struct implements the Executor. In the main function, we have created a variable of Process and passed the Thread value for the Executor field. We have called the Execute method on the exe field of p variable.

9.6.2 Embedding interface into the struct

Like structs, interfaces can also be embedded in the struct. When an interface is embedded in the struct, all the methods of the interface are directly available in the struct. One point needs to be taken care of which is that while creating a value of a struct, we have to pass the actual implementation value of an interface; otherwise, panic will be raised while calling the methods of the interface.

Program 9.14 is almost the same as *Program 9.13*. The difference is that we are embedding the interface here whereas we had used the interface variable as a field in *Program 9.13*. Here, we are calling the interface method directly whereas we had called the interface method on interface field of struct value previously.

Program 9.14

```go
package main

import "fmt"

type Executor interface {
    Execute()
}

type Thread struct {
}

func (t Thread) Execute() {
    fmt.Println("Executing thread")
}
```

```
type Process struct {
    Executor
}


func main() {
    p := Process{Thread{}}
    p.Execute()
}
```

Conclusion

- The methods in an interface do not have a body. All methods of an interface are purely abstract.
- An interface's methods can have arguments and return types.
- Any custom type can implement the interface.
- There is no explicit syntax to implement an interface. When any type defines all methods of the interface, then that type implicitly implements the interface.
- A type that implements an interface can also have other methods.
- A type can implement more than one interface.
- An interface can be implemented by many types.
- When an interface does not have any method, it is called an empty interface. An empty interface is by default implemented by all types.
- An interface can be used as a field of a struct. When it is used, we need to pass the actual implementation of the interface while creating a struct object.
- Polymorphism can be implemented using an interface in Golang.

Questions

1. What will be the result of the following program?

```
package main

import "fmt"

type I interface {
```

```
    m1()
}

type T struct {
}

func (t *T) m1() {
    fmt.Println("M1 of T")
}

func main() {
    var i I
    t := T{}
    i = t
    i.m1()
}
```

a. M1 of T

b. Compilation error

2. What will be the result of the following program?

```
package main

import "fmt"

type I interface {
    m1()
}

type T struct {
}

func (t *T) m1() {
    fmt.Println("M1 of T")
}
func (t *T) m2() {
    fmt.Println("M2 of T")
```

```
}

func main() {
    var i I
    t := T{}
    i = &t
    i.m2()
}
```

   a. M2 of T

   b. M1 of T

   c. Compilation error

3. What is the stringer interface?

   a. It converts every object into a string.

   b. It is an empty interface and every type by default implements this.

   c. It has a method named `String()`. When you implement the `String` method on any type, we can customize the output of the type.

   d. There is no such interface in Golang.

4. Which is the name of the interface which can be used for sorting?

   a. `Sorter`

   b. `SortInterface`

   c. `Comparator`

   d. `Interface`

5. Select true statements from the followings.

   a. The implements key can be used to implement an interface.

   b. A type can implement more than one interface.

   c. An interface can be implemented by many types.

   d. There is no syntax to implement an interface

   e. To implement an interface in any type, the type needs to implement all the methods of the interface.

CHAPTER 10
Pointers

The pointer variable can hold the memory address of another variable. When the value of the variable is changed, it reflects in the pointer variable. Pointers are very useful when the variable is passed to the function. When any change happens to the variable, it reflects in the caller function.

Structure

- What are pointers?
- How can we use pointers?
- Pointer concepts
- Programming examples

Objective

In this chapter, you will learn what pointers are in Golang. This chapter will explain to you the use of a pointer, how to declare a pointer variable, and what are the pointer types. You will also learn why arithmetic operations are not allowed on pointer variables in Golang.

10.1 Declaration

The ampersand (&) can be used to access the memory address of any value. In the program, the address of variable x is accessed using &x and assigned to variable a. *Program 10.1* will print the value and address of the variable x.

```
Program 10.1
package main
import "fmt"
func main() {
    x := 15
    a := &x
    fmt.Println("Value of x:", x)
    fmt.Println("Address of x:", a)
}
```

The following will be the output for the above program:

Value of x: 15

Address of x: 0xc000014058

Note: Memory address of x can be different on each run.

The variable, a, is called a pointer variable because it holds the memory address of a variable. The value of a pointer variable (memory address) can be accessed using an asterisk (*). Accessing the pointer's underlying value using the * is called *dereferencing* or *in directing*. *Program 10.2* will print **15**.

```
Program 10.2
package main

import "fmt"

func main() {
    x := 15
    a := &x
    fmt.Println("Value at address of x:", *a)
}
```

The following will be the output for the above program:

Value at address of x: 15

The above dereferencing statement is equivalent to the statement below:

```
fmt.Println("Value of x:", *(&x))
```

Since the pointer variable holds the address of any value, any modification to the value of the pointer variable will be reflected in the actual value. *Program 10.3* modifies the value of *a and it will reflect in variable x as well.

Program 10.3

```go
package main

import "fmt"

func main() {
    x := 15
    a := &x
    fmt.Println("Value of x(before modification):", x)
    fmt.Println("Value of *a:(before modification):", *a)
    *a = 20
    fmt.Println("Value of x(After modification):", x)
    fmt.Println("Value of *a:(After modification):", *a)
}
```

The following will be the output for the above program:

Value of x(before modification): 15

Value of *a:(before modification): 15

Value of x(After modification): 20

Value of *a:(After modification): 20

The built-in function new( ) can be used to create a pointer:

Program 10.4

```go
package main

import "fmt"
```

```
func main() {
    a := new(int)
    *a = 15
    fmt.Println(*a)
    fmt.Println(a)
}
```

The following will be the output for the above program:

15

0xc000014058

The pointer variable can also be created using the var keyword. The following statements create a pointer of type *int and the assigned address of x to the pointer:

```
x:= 15
var a *int
a = &x
```

10.2 Pointer type

Till now, we have created a pointer variable using := and the type of variable was inferred as *int. We can print the type of variable using the reflect package as shown below:

```
Program 10.5
package main

import (
    "fmt"
    "reflect"
)

func main() {
    x := 15
    a := &x
    fmt.Println(reflect.TypeOf(a))
}
```

The following will be the output for the above program:

```
*int
```

It is also an important point to note that the address of type T can only be assigned to type *T. Violating this rule gives a compilation error. *Program 10.6* will not compile because the address of an int variable is assigned the *float64 variable which is a type mismatch.

```
Program 10.6
package main
func main() {
    x := 15
    var a *float64
    a = &x
}
```

The following will be the output for the above program:

```
Error 10.1: cannot use &x (type *int) as type *float64 in assignment
```

If a pointer variable created using a var keyword has not assigned a memory address, it will point to the nil pointer. If we try to print it, <nil> will be printed on the console.

var a *float64

fmt.Println(*a)

Ques: What will happen if we try to access the value of the <nil> pointer using the asterisk?

Ans: If we try to access the value at nil pointer, the Go program will panic with a runtime error. The following program gives a demonstration:

```
Program 10.7
package main

import "fmt"

func main() {
    var a *float64
    fmt.Println(*a)
```

```
}
```

The following will be the output for the above program:

```
Error 10.2: panic: runtime error: invalid memory address or nil pointer
dereference
[signal SIGSEGV: segmentation violation code=0x1 addr=0x0 pc=0x1091507]
```

10.3 Operators with the pointer

Like C and C++, we can apply operators on a pointer but with limited usage. We can use a relational operator on a pointer in Golang. We cannot use arithmetic or any other operators on pointers.

10.3.1 Relational operator

The only relation operator allowed on pointers is the equality operator. The equality operator can be used to check whether two pointers are pointing to the same memory address or not. This is demonstrated in *Program 10.8*:

```
Program 10.8
package main
import "fmt"
func main() {
    x := 15
    y := 15
    a := &x
    b := &x
    c := &y
    fmt.Println(a == b)
    fmt.Println(a == c)
}
```

The following will be the output for the above program:

true

false

The equality operator (== or !=) can be used to check whether a particular variable has a memory address or nil pointer as shown below:

```
var a *float64
```

```
fmt.Println(a == nil)
```

The following will be the output for the above statements:

```
true
```

10.3.2 Arithmetic operator

Those who are coming from a C/C++ background would expect arithmetic operators on pointers. But for the sake of simplicity, the arithmetic operators are not allowed on pointers in the Go language. The arithmetic operators on pointers may lead to an illegal address which is very dangerous.

In the C family languages, the pointer arithmetic is very useful when iterating over an array because it is very fast. However, the hardware and compiler are so advanced nowadays that iterating arrays using indices is more efficient than using pointer arithmetic. So, there is no need for the pointer arithmetic to perform a fast iteration over the array.

10.4 Pointers on composite types

We have seen pointers on basic data types. Now, we will see the pointer in composite data types like `array`, `struct`, and `slice`.

10.4.1 Pointer to array

We can create a pointer to the array and pass it to the function. When the calling function makes any modification to an array, it will reflect in the caller function. Before understanding how modification is done by calling a function on array that reflects in the caller function, let's first see how to create a pointer to an array.

10.4.1.1 Declaration

There are two ways of creating a pointer to an array: by using the var keyword and by using the := operator.

Declaration using the var keyword

Program 10.9 declares a pointer to the array using the var keyword:

```
Program 10.9
```

```
package main
```

```go
import "fmt"

func main() {
    var arr1 *[5]int
    var arr2 = [5]int{1, 2, 3, 4, 5}
    arr1 = &arr2
    fmt.Println((*arr1)[0])
}
```

The following will be the output for the above program:

```
1
```

In *Program 10.9*, we have declared a pointer to an array variable, arr1, using an asterisk (*). We have declared the array of int, i.e., arr2. Then, we have assigned the address arr2 to arr1. We have printed the zeroth element of arr1. We can see in the output that the zeroth element arr1 is 1 because we have assigned arr2 to arr1 and arr2 has value 1 at the zeroth array location. Please note that we have used an asterisk to access the value on pointer array as *(arr1)[0].

It is not necessary to use an asterisk to access elements on the pointer array. We can access an element of the pointer array, the same as not an array variable. It looks very clear. *Program 10.10* accesses the pointer array element without using an asterisk:

Program 10.10

```go
package main

import "fmt"

func main() {
    var arr1 *[5]int
    var arr2 = [5]int{1, 2, 3, 4, 5}
    arr1 = &arr2
    fmt.Println(arr1[0])
}
```

The following will be the output for the above program:

```
1
```

The output *Program 10.10* is similar to *Program 10.9*. The code is almost similar except for one change, i.e., we are accessing the pointer array element without using an asterisk. It is just arr1[0], not (*arr)[0]. It looks very clear and more readable.

When a pointer array is declared using the var keyword but has not assigned any address of the array and we try to access any element of the pointer array, the program will panic. This is demonstrated in *Program 10.11*:

Program 10.11

```
package main


import "fmt"


func main() {
    var arr1 *[5]int
    fmt.Println(arr1[0])
}
```

The following will be the error in the above program:

Error 10.3

```
panic: runtime error: invalid memory address or nil pointer dereference
[signal SIGSEGV: segmentation violation code=0x1 addr=0x0 pc=0x109d09f]


goroutine 1 [running]:
main.main()
    /Users/prithvipalsingh/go/src/workspace/main.go:7 +0x1f
exit status 2
```

In *Program 10.11*, we have declared the pointer array but we have not assigned the address of the any array. When we run, it panics because we tried to get the zeroth element of the pointer array but there is no underlying array that exists.

Declaration using := operator

Program 10.12 creates the pointer array using the := operator:

Program 10.12

```
package main
```

```go
import "fmt"

func main() {
    var arr2 = [5]int{1, 2, 3, 4, 5}
    arr1 := &arr2
    fmt.Println("Zeroth element of arr1:", arr1[0])
}
```

The following will be the output for the above program:

Zeroth element of arr1: 1

Please note that we have created an array using the var keyword. The pointer array type will be inferred from the right side of the := operator.

10.4.1.2 Pointer array as a function argument

We can pass a pointer array as a function argument. When we modify any element of the pointer array in calling the function, then that change will be reflected in the caller function. In *Program 10.13*, we will modify one array index in the calling function and the new value will be available in the caller function:

Program 10.13

```go
package main

import "fmt"

func main() {
    arr := [5]int{10, 20, 30, 40, 50}
    modify(&arr)
    fmt.Println("Array Elements", arr)
}

func modify(arr *[5]int) {
    arr[0] = 100
}
```

The following will be the output for the above program:

Array Elements [100 20 30 40 50]

In *Program 10.13*, we have initialized the array of int with size 5. We have passed the address of the array into the modify function. In the modify function, we have changed the zeroth element of the array and assigned 100 to it. In the main function, we have printed the array. It prints the array elements mentioned in the output of *Program 10.13*. You can see that the zeroth element of the array is 100 in the main function as well. This means that modification has been done in the calling function which is visible in the caller function.

Note: It is not a good practice to send the address array to the function. We should create a slice from the array with the default indexes and pass the slice in the function.

When we create a slice from the array with default indexes, the start index will be zero and the last index will be the length of the array minus 1. This means that it will create a slice with the whole array, and the underlying data structure of that slice will be an original array. Any modification to the slice will reflect in the original array.

Program 10.14

```
package main

import "fmt"

func main() {
    arr := [5]int{10, 20, 30, 40, 50}
    modify(arr[:])
    fmt.Println("Slice Elements", arr)
}

func modify(arr []int) {
    arr[0] = 100
}
```

The following will be the output for the above program:

Slice Elements [100 20 30 40 50]

In *Program 10.14*, we have defined a function, `modify`, with the slice as an argument. The `modify` function modifies the zeroth element of slice and assigns `100`. In the main function, we have declared an array with the default value. In the next line, we have called the `modify` function. Please note that we have created a slice from the array (using `arr[:]`) and passed to the function. Finally, we have printed the array. We can see in the output of *Program 10.14* that the zeroth element of the array has `100`.

10.4.2 Pointer to slice

We can create a pointer to the slice, but why do we need a pointer to the slice? We have already seen in *Section 9.4.1.3* that if we modify any element of the slice, it will be visible to the caller function. So what is the use of a pointer to a slice?

A pointer to a slice is very frequently used in standard or custom libraries. Let us understand the importance of the pointer to a slice in Golang. As we know, slice is a dynamic data structure. We can append as many elements to a slice as we need. We have seen in *Program 10.14* that when we modify an existing element of the slice in the calling function, it reflects in the caller function. But, when we append new elements to the slice in the calling, it does not reflect in the caller function. Let us see this in *Program 10.15*:

Program 10.15

```
package main


import "fmt"


func main() {
    s1 := []int{10, 20, 30, 40, 50}
    modify(s1)
    fmt.Println("Slice Elements", s1)
}


func modify(s1 []int) {
    s1[0] = 100
    s1 = append(s1, 60)
    s1 = append(s1, 70)
}
```

The following will be the output for the above program:

Slice Elements [100 20 30 40 50]

In *Program 10.15*, we have modified the modify function. Apart from modifying the zeroth element of the slice, we are appending 60 and 70 to the slice. In the main function, we are calling the modify function and printing the slice in the next line. Please note that in the output of *Program 10.15*, the appended values are not printed. Only the zeroth element is changed. This concludes that when the new element is appended to the slice in the calling function, the appended values are not reflected in the caller function.

As slice is a dynamic data structure, it is very important that when the calling function adds new values to the slice, it should be reflected in the caller function as well otherwise, there is no use of adding new value in the slice. This can be achieved using a pointer to the slice.

Program 10.16

```
package main

import "fmt"

func main() {
    s1 := []int{10, 20, 30, 40, 50}
    modify(&s1)
    fmt.Println("Slice Elements", s1)
}

func modify(s1 *[]int) {
    (*s1)[0] = 100
    *s1 = append(*s1, 60)
    *s1 = append(*s1, 70)
}
```

The following will be the output for the above program:

Slice Elements [100 20 30 40 50 60 70]

In *Program 10.16*, we have changed the modify function to take a pointer to the slice as an argument. Now when we run this program, the output will not be the same as the output of *Program 10.15*. We can see that the appended elements are reflected in the main function. So, the pointer to the slice is very useful.

10.4.3 Pointer to struct

A pointer to a struct can be created using ampersand (&). We can access or modify the field of a pointer to a struct variable by using or without using an asterisk. We can assign the address of one struct to the pointer of the struct variable. When any changes are done on the pointer to the struct variable, it will be reflected in the original struct.

Program 10.17

```
package main

import "fmt"

type person struct {
    id   int
    name string
}

func main() {
    p1 := person{101, "XYX"}
    p2 := &p1
    fmt.Println("Person *p2.id:", (*p2).id)
    fmt.Println("Person p2.id:", p2.id)
    p2.name = "ABC"
    fmt.Println("Person p1:", p1)
}
```

The following will be the output for the above program:

Person *p2.id: 101

Person p2.id: 101

Person p1: {101 ABC}

In *Program 10.17*, we have defined a struct named as person with the fields id and name. In the main function, we have created an object of the person struct, i.e., p1.

We have created a pointer to the struct variable p2 and assigned the address of p1 to it. We have two print statements to print the id of the p2 variable. In the first print statement, we have used asterisk whereas in the second print statement, we have not used asterisk. Both the print statements output the same result. In the next line, we have changed the name field of the p2 variable. The changed name field is reflected in p1 because p2 holds the address p1.

A pointer to struct can also be created at the time of struct initialization. We can use an ampersand while initializing the struct:

```
p1 := &person{101, "XYX"}
```

Like array and slice, a pointer to struct can be passed as a function argument. When a calling function changes any field of a pointer to the struct variable, it will be reflected in the calling function.

Program 10.18

```
package main

import "fmt"

type person struct {
    id   int
    name string
}

func main() {
    p1 := &person{101, "XYX"}
    modify(p1)
    fmt.Println("Person p1:", p1)
}

func modify(p1 *person) {
    p1.name = "NewXYZ"
}
```

The following will be the output for the above program:

```
Person p1: &{101 NewXYZ}
```

In *Program 10.18,* the modify function takes the pointer of the person struct as an argument. The modify function changes the name field from XYZ to NewXYZ. In the main function, we have created a pointer to the struct variable p1 and passed it to the modify function. When we print p1, it prints the changed value of the name field.

Conclusion

- A pointer variable can hold the address of another variable.
- The ampersand (&) can be used to access the memory address of the variable.
- The asterisk (*) can be used to access the value at the address.
- The reflect package can be used to find the type of the pointer variable.
- The pointer variable must be assigned with the address of another variable before the access value of the pointer variable, otherwise the code will panic.
- The address of the int variable can only be assigned to the pointer variable type of *int. The same is applicable to other types as well.
- The only relational operator that can be used on the pointer variable is the equality operator.
- We can create a pointer to the array but it is not recommended to use it. We should create a slice from an array and pass it to another function.
- When we want to append values to the slice which is an argument to the function, we must define an argument as a pointer to slice.

Questions

1. What will be the output of the following program?

```go
package main
import "fmt"
type person struct {
    id    int
    name string
}

func main() {
    p1 := &person{101, "XYX"}
    modify(p1)
```

```
    fmt.Println("Person p1:", *p1)
}

func modify(p1 *person) {
    p1 = &person{202, "ABC"}
}
```

a. Person p1: {101 XYX}

b. Person p1: {202 ABC}

2. What will be the result in the following program?

```
package main

import "fmt"

func main() {
    var a *int
    b := 10.3
    a = &b
    fmt.Println(*a)
}
```

a. The program will panic with nil pointer dereferencing error.

b. It will print 10.3.

c. There will be a compilation error because we cannot assign the address of the float variable to the int type pointer variable.

3. Point out the error in the following program:

```
package main

import "fmt"

func main() {
    var a *int
    fmt.Println(*a)
}
```

4. Which of the following statements will return true?

   a.
   ```
   var a *int
   fmt.Println(a == nil)
   ```

   b.
   ```
   var a *int
   var b *int
   fmt.Println(a == b)
   ```

   c.
   ```
   a := 10
   b := 10
   x := &a
   y := &b
   fmt.Println(x == y)
   ```

5. What will be the output of the following program?

   ```
   package main
       import "fmt"

   func main() {
       a := 10
       b := &a
       fmt.Println(a == b)
   }
   ```

   a. true

   b. false

   c. Compilation error

CHAPTER 11
Concurrency

A process is running a computer program that may have multiple threads. When a process runs multiple threads on a single core/processor, it is called a concurrent program. When a process runs multiple threads on multiple cores/processors, it is called a parallelized program. In Golang, we can use goroutines to write a concurrent program and channel for communication between goroutines.

Structure

- Concurrency with goroutines
- Communication between goroutines using channel
- Programming examples

Objectives

This chapter will cover goroutines and channels. You will learn how to define a goroutine, what is WaitGroup, and how to use `WaitGroup` to wait for other goroutines to finish. You will understand the concept of channel. We will use channel for communication between the goroutines. We will create two types of goroutines: buffered and unbuffered.

11.1 Goroutines

The concurrent programs in Golang are called goroutines. Multiple goroutines can run in parallel. Each Go program has at least one goroutine which is called the main goroutine. The main goroutine can spawn any numbers of goroutines.

11.1.1 Introduction

We need to prepend the go keyword before the function call to start the function as a new goroutine, and it will have a separate call stack. The new goroutine will be the child of the main goroutine. When the main ends, the Go runtime terminates all its children's goroutines.

Program 11.1

```go
package main

import (
    "fmt"
    "time"
)

func main() {
    go f1("F1")
    go f1("F2")
    fmt.Println("Sleeping for 5 second")
    time.Sleep(5 * time.Second)
    fmt.Println("Main completed")
}
func f1(name string) {
    for index := 0; index < 10; index++ {
        fmt.Printf("%v: index %d\n", name, index)
        time.Sleep(1 * time.Second)
    }
}
```

The following will be the output for the above program:

```
F1: index 0
F2: index 0
Sleeping for 5 second
F2: index 1
F1: index 1
F2: index 2
F1: index 2
F2: index 3
F1: index 3
F2: index 4
F1: index 4
Main completed
```

Please note that the above output is not predictable. There could be a different output each time we execute this code.

In *Program 11.1*, we have defined a function, f1 with a parameter of string, i.e., name. This function has a for-loop which iterates 10 times from 0 to 9. Within the for-loop, it prints the name and index of the loop and then it sleeps for 1 second. So, for each iteration of for-loop, it sleeps for one second after the print statement.

In the main function, we have called the f1 function twice as the goroutines. These are called as goroutines because we have prepended the go keyword before the function call. We have passed F1 as an argument in the first function call and F2 as an argument to the second call. The main function sleeps for five seconds after calling the goroutines, so the goroutines get some time to execute.

Please note the output of the above code. The goroutine does not print the values of all the iterations. It prints till 4th for both the goroutines and the program ends, whereas we have written for loop to print from 0 to 9. This happened because of each iteration of for-loop sleeping for 1 second. The for-loop iterates 10 times so the total sleep time is 10 seconds. But the main function sleeps only for 5 seconds. So when the main ends, it does not wait for the child goroutine to complete. It terminates the child goroutines when the main goroutine ends. Again, the output is not predictable and it may be a possibility that you'll run this program.

11.1.2 WaitGroup

In the previous section, we have used the Sleep function to wait for child goroutines to finish. But the Sleep function is not a good practice to wait for the child goroutine to finish. We can use WaitGroup of the sync package to wait for the child goroutine to finish.

The sync.WaitGroup is a struct type. It has three useful methods:

- **Add**: The Add method adds an integer number to the WaitGroup. The integer number is a count that says the main function will wait for that number of a goroutine to complete.

- **Done**: The Done method decreases the count, which is added in the Add function. We should call this at the end of the goroutine.

- **Wait**: The Wait method waits for all goroutines to finish. When the count reaches 0, it finishes the wait.

Let's look at the following program:

Program 11.2

```
package main

import (
    "fmt"
    "sync"
    "time"
)

func main() {
    var wg sync.WaitGroup
    wg.Add(2)
    go f1("F1", &wg)
    go f1("F2", &wg)
    fmt.Println("Main: Waiting for Goroutines to finish")
    wg.Wait()
    fmt.Println("Main completed")
}
func f1(name string, wg *sync.WaitGroup) {
```

```
    for index := 0; index < 10; index++ {
        fmt.Printf("%v: index %d\n", name, index)
        time.Sleep(1 * time.Second)
    }
    wg.Done()
}
```

The following will be the output for the above program:

Main: Waiting for Goroutines to finish

F1: index 0

F2: index 0

F2: index 1

F1: index 1

F1: index 2

F2: index 2

F2: index 3

F1: index 3

F2: index 4

F1: index 4

F1: index 5

F2: index 5

F2: index 6

F1: index 6

F1: index 7

F2: index 7

F1: index 8

F2: index 8

F2: index 9

F1: index 9

Main completed

Program 11.2 is almost the same as *Program 11.1*. The only difference here is that we have defined a variable wg of sync.WaitGroup. We have called the Add method and passed 2 as an argument. We have passed the address wg variable to the goroutines.

We have called the same function two times as the goroutine. We have called the Done function wg variable at the end of the function. It means that the execution of the goroutine is complete. We have called the Wait method at the end of the main function.

If all goroutines are completed but in wait, the count has not reached zero, there will be a deadlock in the Wait method. So, the code will panic at the Wait method call. Please try this as an exercise.

11.1.3 Mutex Lock

When multiple goroutines update any shared variable, that scenario is called a race condition. The race condition causes an inconsistent update of shared variables. The code which causes the inconsistently update of the variable is called a critical section. We can use sync. Mutex struct to lock the critical section so that only one goroutine can update the variables:

Program 11.3

```
package main

import (
    "fmt"
    "sync"
)
var amount = 1000
func main() {
    var wg sync.WaitGroup
    wg.Add(100)
    for index := 0; index < 100; index++ {
        go withdraw(&wg)
    }
    wg.Wait()
    fmt.Println(amount)
}


func withdraw(wg *sync.WaitGroup) {
    defer wg.Done()
```

```
        amount = amount - 1
}
```

The output of *Program 11.3* is not predictable. The expected output is 900, but when you run this program, you will get values between `900` to `1000`.

We have executed the withdraw function as 100 goroutines. The `withdraw` function reduces 1 from the amount in each goroutine call. The amount variable is a shared variable, so decrement 1 from the amount is a critical section. We need a wrap decrement statement in the mutex lock. We have done this in *Program 11.4*:

Program 11.4

```
package main

import (
    "fmt"
    "sync"
)

var amount = 1000

func main() {
    var wg sync.WaitGroup
    var m sync.Mutex
    wg.Add(100)
    for index := 0; index < 100; index++ {
        go withdraw(&wg, &m)
    }
    wg.Wait()
    fmt.Println(amount)
}

func withdraw(wg *sync.WaitGroup, m *sync.Mutex) {
    defer wg.Done()
    m.Lock()
```

```
    amount = amount - 1
    m.Unlock()
}
```

The following will be the output for the above program:

900

We have created a variable of `sync.Mutex` in the main method and we have passed its address to the `withdraw` function. We have called `Lock` before the `decrement` statement and `Unlock` after it, so now decrement is safe. It will always give the same result.

A drawback of the Mutex lock: Since it locks for other goroutines to access the critical section, it slows down the overall execution of the program.

11.2 Some important functions

There are some functions available in the Go standard library. We can use those functions to control the execution of the goroutines.

11.2.1 The GOMAXPROCS functions

The Go runtime runs goroutines within a logical processor. One logical processor is bound to one operating system thread. We can specify how many logical processors will be used in a program. We can set a number of logical processors by setting the value to `runtime.GOMAXPROCS()` function. The default value for GOMAXPROCS is 1. It means that multiple goroutines can be mapped on an OS thread.

Adding more values to GOMAXPROCS means adding more logical processors. If we run a program where GOMAXPROCS is 2, and the machine has multiple core/processors, then the program will run parallely. If the machine has a single-core, then the program will run concurrently using multiple threads:

Program 11.5

```
package main

import (
    "fmt"
    "runtime"
    "sync"
```

```
)

func main() {
    runtime.GOMAXPROCS(2)
    var wg sync.WaitGroup
    wg.Add(2)
    go f1("F1", &wg)
    go f1("F2", &wg)
    fmt.Println("Main: Waiting for Goroutines to finish")
    wg.Wait()
    fmt.Println("Main completed")
}
func f1(name string, wg *sync.WaitGroup) {
    for index := 0; index < 10; index++ {
        fmt.Printf("%v: index %d\n", name, index)
    }
    wg.Done()
}
```

The output of *Program 11.5* is not predictable, but it will run parallelly. We have called `runtime.GOMAXPROCS` at the first line of the main function.

11.2.2 The Goexit function

We can use the `Goexit` function to stop the execution of the goroutine. The `Goexit` function will stop a goroutine in which it is called.

Program 11.6

```
package main

import (
    "fmt"
    "runtime"
    "sync"
```

```
)

func main() {
    var wg sync.WaitGroup
    wg.Add(1)
    go f1("F1", &wg)
    fmt.Println("Main: Waiting for Goroutines to finish")
    wg.Wait()
    fmt.Println("Main completed")
}
func f1(name string, wg *sync.WaitGroup) {
    defer wg.Done()
    for index := 0; index < 10; index++ {
        if index == 5 {
            runtime.Goexit()
        }
        fmt.Printf("%v: index %d\n", name, index)
    }
}
```

The following will be the output for the above program:

```
Main: Waiting for Goroutines to finish
F1: index 0
F1: index 1
F1: index 2
F1: index 3
F1: index 4
Main completed
```

In *Program 11.6*, we have executed the f1 function as a goroutine. The f1 function has a for loop iterating from 0 to 10. Within the for loop, we have a condition that if an index value is 5, we call the Goexit function. So, the for loop executes till index 0 to 5 and it exists and prints from 0 to 4. The main function waits until the f1 function completes.

11.3 Channels

Channel is a type in Golang by which two goroutines can communicate. One goroutine can send data and another goroutine can receive data. It is like a pipeline. Channels in Golang introduce a new way of concurrency. The implementation of concurrency using channels works as said in the statement given below:

Do not communicate by sharing memory; instead, share memory by communicating.

We have seen it in *Section 11.1.3* where we used amount as a shared variable, and multiple goroutines were accessing it. The Golang does not encourage concurrency implementation in this way. It strongly says that *do not communicate by sharing memory*. It suggests we should use channels wherever communication is required.

11.3.1 Introduction

The `make` built-in function can be used to declare a channel.

```
make(chan <type>, <buffer size>)
```

- `chan`: A keyword is used for channel declaration.
- `type`: The type is any valid type and the channel will hold values of that type. A type could be a basic data type or a custom type.
- `buffer size`: This is an optional value. The default value is 0. We can declare a buffered channel by providing value. We will discuss buffered and unbuffered channels later in this chapter.

Let's declare a channel that can host integer values.

```
ch := make(chan int)
```

The `<-` operator is used to write and read a value from the channel.

```
ch <- 10
```

The previous statement writes `10` to the channel `ch`.

```
a := <-ch
```

The previous statement reads the value from the channel and stores it to variable `a`.

Let's put it all together. We will write a program that will define a channel, a goroutine will write a value to the channel, and the main method will read the value from the channel.

```
Program 11.7
```

```
package main

import (
    "fmt"
)

func main() {
    ch := make(chan int, 0)
    go writeVal(ch)
    a := <-ch
    fmt.Println(a)
}

func writeVal(ch chan int) {
    ch <- 10
}
```

The following will be the output for the above program:

10

We have defined a channel of int type in the main function. We have called the writeVal function as the goroutine and passed the channel variable to it. In the main function, we are reading the value from the channel, assigning to variable a, and printing the value of a. Please note that read value in the main function will be blocked until the wrtieVal function writes in the channel. So, the main function will be waiting for the value to be available on the channel.

Since read and write operations are blocking calls in the above code, if the main function is waiting for the read from the channel and there is no goroutine that exists, the Go runtime will find it as deadlock and the program will panic. This can be seen in *Program 11.8*:

Program 11.8

```
package main

import (
    "fmt"
```

```
)

func main() {
    ch := make(chan int, 0)
    a := <-ch
    fmt.Println(a)
}
```

The following will be the output for the above program:

```
fatal error: all goroutines are asleep - deadlock!

goroutine 1 [chan receive]:
main.main()
        /Users/prithvipalsingh/PRITHVI/Github/src/go-practice/main.go:9 +0x5b
exit status 2
```

Figure 11.1

Note: It is very important to understand that read and send operations in the channel are atomic.

11.3.2 Operations on channel

We can perform operations on channels. We can close the channels and iterate over the channels. These operations are very frequently used in channels.

11.3.2.1 Closing the channel

We can close a channel using the `close` built-in function. When the channel is closed, we cannot send data to the channel. If we try to perform send operations on the closed channel, the code will panic:

Program 11.9

```
package main

import (
    "fmt"
    "sync"
)
```

```go
func main() {
    var wg sync.WaitGroup
    wg.Add(1)
    ch := make(chan int)
    close(ch)
    go writeVal(ch, &wg)
    wg.Wait()
}


func writeVal(ch chan int, wg *sync.WaitGroup) {
    ch <- 10
    wg.Done()
}
```

The following will be the error in the above program:

panic: send on closed channel

goroutine 19 [running]:
main.writeVal(0xc000094060, 0xc000098000)
    /Users/prithvipalsingh/go/src/workspace/main.go:17 +0x37
created by main.main
    /Users/prithvipalsingh/go/src/workspace/main.go:12 +0xa5
exit status 2

In *Program 11.9,* we have closed the channel after creating it. We have passed the closed channel into the `writeVal()` function. When the send operation is executed in the `writeVal` function, the program panics because the send/write operation is not allowed on the closed channel. We have `WaitGroup` to wait in the main function, so the main does not complete before the `writeVal` goroutine gets a chance to start.

The read operation can be performed on the closed channel. When we perform a read operation on a closed channel, it always returns a zero value. The zero value can be a valid value in the channel. We can differentiate whether the zero value returned from the channel is actually a zero value that exists in the channel or it is because of a closed channel. The channel returns two values: the first is a value and the second is a check for whether the channel is closed or not. When a channel is closed, we will receive that the second value is false:

```
Program 11.10
package main

import (
    "fmt"
)


func main() {
    ch := make(chan int)
    close(ch)
    val, ok := <-ch
    if !ok {
        fmt.Printf("Value %v is returned. the channel is closed\n", val)
    }
}
```

The following will be the output for the above program:

```
Value 0 is returned. the channel is closed
```

11.3.2.2 Iterating over the channel

We can iterate over the channel while reading the channel. There are two ways to iterate over the channel to read data. One way is that we can use the second returned value from the channel. We can use the infinite for-loop to iterate and break when the second value is false. The other way is that we can use the range cause.

Program 11.11 demonstrates the first way:

```
Program 11.11
package main
import "fmt"


func main() {

    ch := make(chan int)
    go func() {
```

```
    for i := 0; i < 10; i++ {
        ch <- i
    }
    close(ch)
  }()

  for {
      val, ok := <-ch
      if !ok {
          break
      }
      fmt.Println(val)
  }
}
```

The following will be the output for the above program:

```
0
1
2
3
4
5
6
7
8
9
```

Program 11.11 can be refactored and the reading code can be minimized:

```
Program 11.12
package main

import "fmt"
```

```go
func main() {

    ch := make(chan int)

    go func() {
        for i := 0; i < 10; i++ {
            ch <- i
        }
        close(ch)
    }()

    for val, ok := <-ch; ok; val, ok = <-ch {
        fmt.Println(val)
    }
}
```

The following will be the output for the above program:

```
0
1
2
3
4
5
6
7
8
9
```

We have refactored the for-loop. We have read the value and ok in the initialization section of for-loop. We are checking the value of the ok variable in the condition section, and reading the value and ok in the postcondition again.

The second way is using the range clause. This is the best way because we don't need a condition and when the channel is closed and all the values of the channel are read, the range cause ends automatically:

Program 11.13

```go
package main

import "fmt"

func main() {

    ch := make(chan int)

    go func() {
        for i := 0; i < 10; i++ {
            ch <- i
        }
        close(ch)
    }()

    for val := range ch {
        fmt.Println(val)
    }
}
```

The following will be the output for the above program:

```
0
1
2
3
4
5
6
7
8
9
```

11.3.3 Types of channels

There are two types of channels: unbuffered and buffered. When we declare a channel without specifying capacity, it will be declared as an unbuffered channel. When we declare a channel with capacity, it will be declared as the buffered channel.

11.3.3.1 Unbuffered channel

When there is no capacity in a channel, then that channel called an unbuffered channel. In the unbuffered channel, the send operation will be blocked until one goroutine reads. The same applies for the read operation. The read operation blocks until one goroutine sends data to it.

Let's write a producer-consumer program and see that the read operation will only be executed when one goroutine writes a value to the channel.

Program 11.14

```
package main

import (
    "fmt"
)

func main() {

    ch := make(chan int)
    done := make(chan bool)
    go producer(ch, done)
    go consumer(ch)
    <-done
}

func producer(ch chan int, done chan bool) {
    for index := 0; index < 10; index++ {
        fmt.Printf("PRODUCER: sending %v\n", index)
        ch <- index
```

```
    }
    close(ch)
    done <- true
}

func consumer(ch chan int) {
    for val := range ch {
        fmt.Printf("CONSUMER: read %v\n", val)
    }


}
```

The following will be the output for the above program:

PRODUCER: sending 0

PRODUCER: sending 1

CONSUMER: read 0

CONSUMER: read 1

PRODUCER: sending 2

PRODUCER: sending 3

CONSUMER: read 2

CONSUMER: read 3

PRODUCER: sending 4

PRODUCER: sending 5

CONSUMER: read 4

CONSUMER: read 5

PRODUCER: sending 6

PRODUCER: sending 7

CONSUMER: read 6

CONSUMER: read 7

PRODUCER: sending 8

PRODUCER: sending 9

CONSUMER: read 8

CONSUMER: read 9

Please note the output of *Program 11.14*. The producer waits until the consumer reads a value from the channel and vice versa. We can see read and send two consecutive times because by the time the consumer prints after reading, the producer prints the send message even though it did not send. The same happened when the producer had already sent one value, printed the second value, and blocked to send a second value, and when the consumer read the first time and printed it, the producer had already printed the next value. So, the producer sends the second value and then the consumer reads and prints. That is the reason we see two times print for producer and consumer.

11.3.3.2 Buffered channel

The buffered channels are those channels that are created with capacity. E.g.:

```
ch := make(chan int, 5)
```

In the buffered channel, the write operation is blocked when the capacity/buffer of the channel is full. In the above statement, when five values are already there in the channel and when we try to send the 6th value, it will be blocked because there will be no space available.

The read operation is blocked when the channel is empty.

Let's write the producer-consumer problem again with the buffered channel:

```
Program 11.15
package main

import (
    "fmt"
)

func main() {

    ch := make(chan int, 5)
    done := make(chan bool)
    go producer(ch, done)
    go consumer(ch)
    <-done
```

```
}


func producer(ch chan int, done chan bool) {
    for index := 0; index < 10; index++ {
        fmt.Printf("PRODUCER: sending %v\n", index)
        ch <- index
    }
    close(ch)
    done <- true
}


func consumer(ch chan int) {
    for val := range ch {
        fmt.Printf("CONSUMER: read %v\n", val)
    }


}
```

The following will be the output for the above program:

PRODUCER: sending 0

PRODUCER: sending 1

PRODUCER: sending 2

PRODUCER: sending 3

PRODUCER: sending 4

PRODUCER: sending 5

PRODUCER: sending 6

CONSUMER: read 0

CONSUMER: read 1

CONSUMER: read 2

CONSUMER: read 3

CONSUMER: read 4

CONSUMER: read 5

CONSUMER: read 6

```
PRODUCER: sending 7
PRODUCER: sending 8
PRODUCER: sending 9
```

Please note the output of *Program11.15*. The producer is not blocked until the length of the channel is 5. The consumer reads 5 values continuously, and then it is blocked because the channel is empty.

11.4 Read-only and send-only channel

We can define a read-only or send-only channel variable as a function parameter. If a function has a read-only channel and we try to send data into that channel, the program will give a compilation error and vice-versa is the same:

```
func readVal(ch <-chan int) {
    ch <- 10
}
```

The above code will give a compilation error because the ch variable is declared as a read-only variable.

Now let's declare a send only channel as a function parameter and see what happens when we receive the value from it.

```
func writeVal(ch chan<- int) {
    <-ch
}
```

Again, the above code will not compile because we are trying to read from the send-only channel.

11.5 Select statement

The select statement is used when there are multiple goroutines that send data in multiple channels. We need to process values from all the channels concurrently. The syntax of the select statement is almost similar to the switch statement. There can be multiple cases within a select statement. Each case statement can have a channel operation. When a case statement can receive from the channel, then that case will be executed. Like the switch statement, the select can also have the default. When none of the cases receive from the channel, then the default section gets executed. The select statement is mostly used in the for-loop but it not necessary:

```go
Program 11.16
package main

import (
    "fmt"
    "time"
)

func main() {
    ch1 := make(chan string)
    ch2 := make(chan string)
    go producer(ch1, "P1", time.Millisecond*1000)
    go producer(ch2, "P2", time.Millisecond*1300)
    receiver(ch1, ch2)
}

func receiver(ch1 chan string, ch2 chan string) {
    for {
        select {
            case msg, ok := <-ch1:
                fmt.Println("Message from ch1", msg)
                if !ok {
                    return
                }
            case msg, ok := <-ch2:
                fmt.Println("Message from ch2", msg)
            if !ok {
                return
            }
        }
    }
}
```

```
func producer(ch chan string, name string, sleep time.Duration) {
    for index := 0; index < 10; index++ {
        time.Sleep(sleep)
        ch <- fmt.Sprintf("%v: %v", name, index)
    }
    close(ch)
}
```

The following will be the output for the above program:

```
Message from ch1 P1: 0
Message from ch2 P2: 0
Message from ch1 P1: 1
Message from ch2 P2: 1
Message from ch1 P1: 2
Message from ch2 P2: 2
Message from ch1 P1: 3
Message from ch1 P1: 4
Message from ch2 P2: 3
Message from ch1 P1: 5
Message from ch2 P2: 4
Message from ch1 P1: 6
Message from ch2 P2: 5
Message from ch1 P1: 7
Message from ch1 P1: 8
Message from ch2 P2: 6
Message from ch1 P1: 9
Message from ch1
```

In *Program 11.16*, we have created two channels, ch1 and ch2, in the main function. We have created a function, i.e., producer. The producer function takes three parameters: channel of string, name as a string, and sleep as Duration. The producer function has a for loop which iterates 10 times and it closes the channel when the for loop finishes. In each iteration, it sleeps for the given sleep duration as a parameter and sends a string as name: index to the channel. In the main function, we have called the producer function as a goroutine two times. The first time we have called producer with ch1, P1 as name and 1000 milliseconds as sleep time. The second time we have called the producer function with ch2, P2 as name and 1300 milliseconds as sleep time.

We have created a function, i.e., receiver. The receiver function takes two channels variable as parameters. It has an infinite for-loop and within the for-loop, we have a select statement with two cases. Both the case statements read from channels. The first case reads from ch1 and the second case reads from ch2. Once read, these case statements print the value and check the ok variable has false. If the ok variable has false value, it returns.

When we run this program, the receiver function reads the value from that channel which has any value. When the channel closed and the case gets ok as false, then the program ends.

11.6 Channels in the time package

There are two channels in the time package: Ticker and Timer. Both are struct and have a channel of Time as a field.

11.6.1 Ticker

The Ticker sends continuous events in the given time. We use Ticker when we need continuous events in a certain time.

We can declare a Ticker by the NewTicker function of time package:

```
ticker := time.NewTicker(time.Millisecond * 1000)
```

We can read events from the channel of the ticker, i.e., C using <- operator:

```
msg := <-ticker.C
```

We can close the channel of Ticker by calling the Stop method on the ticker variable. When we stop a Ticker, the Ticker stops sending events:

```
ticker.Stop()
```

Let's write a program and put whatever we have discussed above all together. This program is almost similar to the program that we have written in *Section 11.5*:

```
Program 11.17

package main


import (
```

```go
    "fmt"
    "time"
)


func main() {
    ticker1 := time.NewTicker(time.Millisecond * 1000)
    ticker2 := time.NewTicker(time.Millisecond * 1300)
    go receiver(ticker1, ticker2)
    time.Sleep(time.Millisecond * 3000)
    ticker1.Stop()
    time.Sleep(time.Millisecond * 10000)
}


func receiver(ticker1 *time.Ticker, ticker2 *time.Ticker) {
    for {
        select {
            case msg := <-ticker1.C:
                fmt.Println("Message from ticker1", msg)
            case msg := <-ticker2.C:
                fmt.Println("Message from ticker2", msg)

        }

    }

}
```

In *Program 11.17*, we have declared two ticker variables: ticker1 and ticker2. ticker1 send events every 1000 milliseconds, and ticker2 send events every 1300 milliseconds. We have called the receiver function as a goroutine. The receiver function has a for-loop. There is a select statement within the for-loop. The select statement has two cases. Each case reads from timer1 and timer2 respectively and prints the returned value. The main function waits for 3000 milliseconds and calls the Stop method on ticker1. Since ticker1 is closed, the first case stops receiving events. The main function waits for 10000 milliseconds again to give a goroutine to execute for some time.

11.6.2 Timer

The Timer is similar to the Ticker, but one difference: the Timer sends an event for only one time, whereas Ticker sends events continuously.

We can declare a Timer by the NewTimer function of the time package. The NewTimer function takes duration as a parameter:

```
timer := time.NewTimer(1000 * time.Millisecond)
```

We can read a value from Timer using the <- operator:

```
<-timer.C
```

We can use the Timer in place of sleep. There is a benefit of using Timer of Sleep which is that we can stop a Timer. So, it will not receive any event at a given time. We can stop a Timer using the Stop method:

```
timer.Stop()
```

We cannot read a value from Timer more than once. If we do that, the program will panic.

Conclusion

- Goroutines can be used to write concurrent programs in Golang.
- When multiple goroutines execute at the same time, their sequence is not predictable. Any goroutine can start first or any goroutine can finish first.
- When the main goroutine exits, all its children also exit.
- If we want the parent goroutine to wait for the child goroutine to finish, then we use WaitGroup to control this.
- The WaitGroup type has three useful methods: Add, Done, and Wait.
- We can use MutexLock to protect a critical section so only one goroutine enters into the critical section.
- We can use a channel for communication between two goroutines.
- The <- operator can be used to send/read the message into/from the channel.
- When a channel is closed, we cannot send more messages to the channel.
- We can use the range clause to read messages from the channel. When the channel is closed and all messages are read, the for loop ends.
- There are two types of channels: buffered and unbuffered.
- While defining the channel as a function argument, we can define read-only or write-only channels.

- The `select` statement can be used when communication happens between multiple channels.

Questions

1. Write a producer-consumer program where there are two producer goroutines that produce data `int` at different intervals. One goroutine will produce data every 300 milliseconds and another goroutine will produce data every 400 milliseconds. There will be one consumer goroutine that will consume the data. Please note that producers should produce data 100 times only.

2. Find an error in the following program:

```
package main

import (
    "fmt"
    "sync"
)

func main() {
    wg := sync.WaitGroup{}
    wg.Add(2)
    go func() {
      fmt.Println("Running go routine")
      wg.Done()
    }()
    wg.Wait()
}
```

3. What is the difference between buffered and unbuffered channels?

4. Which of the following code defines a real-only channel as a function argument?

    a. `func read(ch <-chan int) {`

    `    ch <- 10`

    `    }`

    b. `func read(ch chan<- int) {`

    `    ch <- 10`

    `    }`

c.
```
func read(ch chan int) {
    ch <- 10
}
```

d.
```
func read(<-ch chan int) {
    ch <- 10
}
```

5. What will happen when data is sent to an unbuffered channel but there is no goroutine to read that data?

   a. The program will be stuck for an infinite time.

   b. The program will panic because it is a deadlock.

   c. The program will end whether or not there is a listener.

CHAPTER 12

Error handling

Most of the languages call unexpected behavior as an exception. When exceptions are thrown, we need to handle these exceptions gracefully using the `try/catch` block. The piece of code which causes an exception is called a critical block. The critical block of code which can cause an error needs to be in the `try/catch` block. In Golang, unexpected behavior is called error. Go uses a different approach to handle errors.

Structure

- Error interface
- Panicking and recover
- Best practices for error handling
- Programming examples

Objective

This chapter will cover error handling. At the end of this chapter, you will learn what an error in Golang is, how to return an error from a function or method, and how to handle these errors in the caller function. We will also see a built-in error interface, the error packages and method, function, and struct in the errors package. You will learn how to define a new error, create a customized error type, what panic is, how to handle panic using `recover`, what `defer` is, and the importance of `defer` function while handling panic.

12.1 The error

Go has a built-in error type. The error can be assigned to a variable and returned from a function. *Section 12.1.1* explains the error interface in more detail. Any method / function in Go which may cause unexpected behavior returns the error as the last returned value.

We have already seen in *Section 2.3.1* that a function can return multiple values. When we say the last returned value as an error, it means a function returns multiple values and the last value is an error. It is not mandatory to return an error as the last return value but it is a convention.

There are many functions in the standard library which return the error. One example is `os.Open` as shown below which opens a file and returns `*File` and `error`. If something goes wrong like file not found or you do not have permission to open a file, this function would return an error value; otherwise, it will return file handler as a first return value and nil value for error as a second return value:

```go
func Open(name string) (*File, error) {
    return OpenFile(name, O_RDONLY, 0)
}
```

The caller of this function can check whether the error returned by the function is nil or not before processing the opened file. If an error is not nil, it means there is an error and we cannot proceed further:

```go
file, err := os.Open("myfile.txt")
if err != nil {
    log.Fatal(err)
}
```

Sometimes a function may not return any meaningful value but it may cause an error. In that case, the function will only return an error. One example is the `Mkdir` function of `os` package as shown below:

```go
func Mkdir(name string, perm FileMode) error
```

12.1.1 The error interface

Go has a built-in interface called error which has only one method, i.e., `Error()`. The `Error` method returns string type is as shown below:

```
type error interface {

    Error() string

}
```

Go has a package called `errors`. The `errors` package has an un-exported `errorString` struct type. The `errorString` is an implementation of the error interface because it implements the `Error()` method. The code snippet given below is the full code of the error package:

```
package errors


func New(text string) error {

    return &errorString{text}

}


type errorString struct {

    s string

}


func (e *errorString) Error() string {

    return e.s

}
```

The `errorString` is the most commonly used implementation of the error interface. Since it is unexported, we cannot create a value of `errorString` directly. We need to call the `New()` function to create a value of the `errorString` type as shown below:

```
err := errors.New("Invalid Inputs")
```

The `fmt` package can also be used to create error value. The `Errorf` function uses the `errors.New()` function to create error and `Sprintf` to format the string. The `Errorf` function of the `fmt` package is beneficial to format the error message. It returns the error value as shown below:

```
err := fmt.Errorf("Invalid Input: %v", 12)
```

The create() function in *Program 12.1* creates value for student type, puts in the map, and returns the id of the student. If the name is empty or age is <= 0, it returns an error. The main() function gets the returned values in the id, err variable. It checks the value for the err variable if it is not nil, then it prints the error message and returns. If err is nil, it means there is no error returned from the create() function, so it goes ahead and processes the rest of the code. This code uses the Errorf function of the fmt package to create error value:

Program 12.1

```go
package main

import "fmt"

func main() {
    id, err := create("John", 10)
    if err != nil {
        fmt.Println("Error while creating student")
        fmt.Println(err)
        return
    }
    fmt.Println("Student created with Id=", id)
}

type student struct {
    id   int
    name string
    age  int
}

var stuMap = make(map[int]student)

func create(name string, age int) (int, error) {
    if name == "" {
```

```
        return 0, fmt.Errorf("Invalid Name, Name can't be Empty")
    } else if age <= 0 {
        return 0, fmt.Errorf("Invalid Age %v, Age can't be <= 0", age)
    }
    id := len(stuMap) + 1
    stu := student{id, name, age}
    stuMap[id] = stu
    return id, nil
}
```

Please try this code by passing different values in the create() function and see the output.

12.1.2 User-defined custom error

The custom error can also be created by implementing the error interface. We have previously seen that error interface has only one method, i.e., Error. The following code snippet creates InvalidAgeError:

Code Snippet 12.1

```
type InvalidAgeError struct {
    age int
}
func (i InvalidAgeError) Error() string {
    return fmt.Sprintf("Invalid Age %v, Age can't be <= 0", i.age)
}
```

Now, we can return InvalidAgeError in *Program 12.1* instead of a generic error. *Code Snippet 12.2* shows how we can change the else if part of *Program 12.1*:

Code Snippet 12.2

```
    if name == "" {
        return 0, fmt.Errorf("Invalid Name, Name can't be Empty")
    } else if age <= 0 {
        return 0, InvalidAgeError{age}
    }
```

User-defined errors are instrumental in taking different actions based on the different error types. A function can return different types of errors based on different scenarios. The caller function can assert error type to check the error type and control the flow of the program. We can get values from the asserted error type. *Code Snippet 12.3* shows how to check the error type and get value from the assert type:

```
Code Snippet 12.3

id, err := create("", 10)

if ageError, ok := err.(InvalidAgeError); ok {
    fmt.Println("This is InvalidAgeError. Age:", ageError.age)
    //Take action for InvalidAgeError
} else if nameError, ok := err.(InvalidNameError); ok {
    fmt.Println("This is InvalidNameError. Name:", nameError.name)
    //Take action for InvalidNameError
}
```

12.2 Panic

The unexpected runtime error stops the execution flow of the program abruptly. The most common examples of panic are divide by zero, index out of range, etc. When panic is encountered, the program terminates, deferred functions are called, and control goes to the caller. This process continues till the control reaches the first method of the goroutine call stack.

Finally, it prints the stack trace on the console:

```
Program 12.2

package main


import "fmt"


func main() {
    fmt.Println("Dividing by Zero")
    a := 10
    b := 0
        c := a / b
    fmt.Println("Result:", c)
```

```
}
```

We will get the following error for the above program:

Error 12.1

Dividing by Zero

panic: runtime error: integer divide by zero

goroutine 1 [running]:

main.main()

   /Users/prithvipalsingh/go/src/workspace/main.go:9 +0x7a

exit status 2

The above code does not print the last line. Instead, it panics and stops the program flow with a message. The message shows the reason for the panic, goroutine name, and full-stack trace with file names and line numbers.

It is possible to generate panic explicitly. The built-in panic function can be used to raise a panic explicitly:

Program 12.3

```
package main

import "fmt"

func main() {
    fmt.Println("Start of Main Func")
    fn()
    fmt.Println("End of Main Func")
}
func fn() {
    fmt.Println("Start of fn Func")
    panic("Calling panic explicitly")
    fmt.Println("End of fn Func")
}
```

We will get the following error for the above program:

Error 12.2

```
Start of Main Func
Start of fn Func
panic: Calling panic explicitly

goroutine 1 [running]:
main.fn()
    /Users/prithvipalsingh/go/src/workspace/main.go:12 +0x95
main.main()
    /Users/prithvipalsingh/go/src/workspace/main.go:7 +0x7e
exit status 2
```

In *Program 12.3*, we have defined a function called fn. In the fn function, we have printed a string, called the panic function and then, we have printed again at the end. In the main function, we are printing a string on the console, called the fn function and then we have printed a string at the end. When we run this program, the program panics in the second line of the fn function. In the output of the program, we can see that only the start of the print statement is executed. In contrast, end print statements are not executed because once a panic is raised, the program exits abruptly and nothing will execute after the panic.

Note: Any good editor/IDE will give a warning for the last line of the fn function because it is not reachable.

12.2.1 Panic and defer

Till now, we have seen that when a program panics, the program flow stops and prints a stack trace. We have also seen the defer function in *Section 2.6*. The defer executes at the end of the function call. If there are any defer functions in the call stack, then all defer functions of all the functions in the call stack will be called before the program stops the execution.

The program given below has four functions: main, fn1, fn2, fn3. Each function has a deferred function. When the program panics in function fn3, it executes all the defer functions in reverse order and prints the output on the console before the program stops. Also, note that it does not print the last line of all the functions:

Program 12.4

```
package main
```

```go
import "fmt"

func main() {
    fmt.Println("Start of Main Func")
    defer func() { fmt.Println("Defer in Main func") }()
    fn1()
    fmt.Println("End of Main Func")
}
func fn1() {
    fmt.Println("Start of Fn1 Func")
    defer func() { fmt.Println("Defer in Fn1 func") }()
    fn2()
    fmt.Println("End of Fn1 Func")
}
func fn2() {
    fmt.Println("Start of Fn2 Func")
    defer func() { fmt.Println("Defer in Fn2 func") }()
    fn3()
    fmt.Println("End of Fn2 Func")
}

func fn3() {
    fmt.Println("Start of Fn3 Func")
    defer func() { fmt.Println("Defer in Fn3 func") }()
    panic("Calling panic explicitly in Fn3")
}
```

We will get the following error for the above program:

Error 12.3

Start of Main Func

Start of Fn1 Func

Start of Fn2 Func

Start of Fn3 Func

```
Defer in Fn3 func
Defer in Fn2 func
Defer in Fn1 func
Defer in Main func
panic: Calling panic explicitly in Fn3

goroutine 1 [running]:
main.fn3()
    /Users/prithvipalsingh/go/src/workspace/main.go:27 +0xb7
main.fn2()
    /Users/prithvipalsingh/go/src/workspace/main.go:20 +0xa0
main.fn1()
    /Users/prithvipalsingh/go/src/workspace/main.go:14 +0xa0
main.main()
    /Users/prithvipalsingh/go/src/workspace/main.go:8 +0xa0
exit status 2
```

12.3 Recover

The built-in function `recover` recovers from panic. The program usually executes after the recover call. It should be called from the `defer` function; otherwise, it will not have any impact.

The `recover` function can be called from any function in the call stack. It is not necessary to call the `recover` function the same function from where panic is encountered. In the code given below, the recover function is called in the `fn2` function. After the `fn2` call, the program doesn't terminate. Instead, it regains the flow and ends the program gracefully. It is important to note that the last line of `fn2` doesn't execute:

Program 12.5

```go
package main

import "fmt"

func main() {
    fmt.Println("Start of Main Func")
```

```go
    defer func() { fmt.Println("Defer in Main func") }()
    fn1()
    fmt.Println("End of Main Func")
}
func fn1() {
    fmt.Println("Start of Fn1 Func")
    defer func() { fmt.Println("Defer in Fn1 func") }()
    fn2()
    fmt.Println("End of Fn1 Func")
}
func fn2() {
    fmt.Println("Start of Fn2 Func")
    defer func() {
        fmt.Println("Defer in Fn2 func")
        if rec := recover(); rec != nil {
            fmt.Println("Recovered:", rec)
        }
    }()
    fn3()
    fmt.Println("End of Fn2 Func")
}
func fn3() {
    fmt.Println("Start of Fn3 Func")
    defer func() { fmt.Println("Defer in Fn3 func") }()
    panic("Calling panic explicitly in Fn3")
}
```

We will get the following output for the above program:

Start of Main Func

Start of Fn1 Func

Start of Fn2 Func

Start of Fn3 Func

Defer in Fn3 func

Defer in Fn2 func

Recovered: Calling panic explicitly in Fn3

End of Fn1 Func

Defer in Fn1 func

End of Main Func

Defer in Main func

The recover function returns nil if there is no panic in the call stack. This is demonstrated in *Program 12.6*:

Program 12.6

```go
package main

import "fmt"

func main() {
    fmt.Println("Start of Main Func")
    defer func() { fmt.Println("Defer in Main func") }()
    fn1()
    fmt.Println("End of Main Func")
}
func fn1() {
    fmt.Println("Start of Fn1 Func")
    defer func() {
        fmt.Println("Defer in Fn1 func")
        fmt.Println("Recovered:", recover())
    }()
    fmt.Println("End of Fn1 Func")
}
```

We will get the following output for the above program:

Start of Main Func

Start of Fn1 Func

End of Fn1 Func

```
Defer in Fn1 func
Recovered: <nil>
End of Main Func
Defer in Main func
```

Program 12.7 shows that if the recover function is called without the defer function, it will not have any impact and it will always return nil:

```
Program 12.7
package main

import "fmt"

func main() {
    fmt.Println("Start of Main Func")
    defer func() { fmt.Println("Defer in Main func") }()
    fn1()
    fmt.Println("End of Main Func")
}
func fn1() {
    fmt.Println("Start of Fn1 Func")
    fmt.Println("Recovered", recover())
    defer func() {
        fmt.Println("Defer in Fn1 func")
    }()
    panic("Panicing from fn1")
}
```

We will get the following output for the above program:

```
Start of Main Func
Start of Fn1 Func
Recovered <nil>
Defer in Fn1 func
Defer in Main func
```

```
panic: Panicing from fn1

goroutine 1 [running]:
main.fn1()
    /Users/prithvipalsingh/go/src/workspace/main.go:17 +0x147
main.main()
    /Users/prithvipalsingh/go/src/workspace/main.go:8 +0xa0
exit status 2
```

12.4 Best practice

It is not a good practice to call panic explicitly in program logic. The caller of your function will not know that your function can panic and so, the caller may not write the recover function. In that case, the whole program will terminate. It is always the best practice to return an error from the function instead of calling panic explicitly.

When a function returns an error, we should handle that error. We should not ignore it.

Conclusion

- Golang uses error type for error handling.
- A function can return an error type as the last return type if the function can cause the error.
- It not mandatory to return error type as the last return type. It is a convention.
- When there is no error returned by the function, the function returns nil as an error. The caller function checks whether the error is nil or not to check if there is an error in calling the function.
- We can create customized error by implementing the `Error()` method of the error interface.
- If there is an unexpected behavior, the Golang code panics. An example of expected behavior is accessing an array element by index more than length.
- The `recover` function can be used to handle panic.

Questions

1. Which of the following is the constructor method to create a new error object?

   a. `New()`

   b. `NewErr()`

   c. `NewError()`

   d. `Err()`

2. Modify the following code so this program will finish gracefully by print error. Note: Don't modify the array index.

   ```
   package main
   import "fmt"

   func main() {
       arr := [5]int{10, 20, 30, 40, 50}
       index := 5
       fmt.Println(arr[index])
   }
   ```

3. Which method do we need to define to create a custom error type?

   a. `Error()`

   b. `Errors()`

   c. `Err()`

   d. `NewErr()`

4. Which of the following statements is true about defer?

   a. Defer function executes when the whole call stack is finished

   b. Defer function executes at the end of the parent function. When the parent function finishes its execution, only then the `defer` function executes.

   c. Defer function executes at the start of the parent function.

   d. Defer function only runs when there is an error in the parent function.

5. Is it necessary to call the recover function in the defer function?

   a. Yes

   b. No

Index

Made in the USA
Monee, IL
11 November 2021